FROM PYRAMID TO PILLAR
Population change and social security in Europe

FROM PYRAMID TO PILLAR

Population change and social security in Europe

INTERNATIONAL LABOUR OFFICE   GENEVA

ISBN 92-2-106456-5 (limp cover)
ISBN 92-2-106497-2 (hard cover)

First published 1989

Photocomposed in India/Printed in Switzerland   MAC/VAU

CONTENTS

Figures

Tables

Contents

Tables in statistical appendix

INTRODUCTION

The influence of demographic factors on the development of social security in the highly industrialised countries—especially the European ones—or at any rate the way this influence is viewed by public opinion and by specialised circles, is becoming more apparent and increasingly significant as time passes. This is especially the case since almost all European countries must be prepared from now on to cope with the repercussions of the unprecedented concurrence of two trends. First, the population of Europe is ageing, in so far as the proportion of older people—whatever the definition applied—is growing steadily and, in many cases, spectacularly. Second, there is a drop (often a steady one) in the birth rates of these same countries, at least in most of them, and usually it is no longer possible to take remedial steps. In the past these steps consisted either of stringent measures to combat infant mortality—which is now extremely low in many countries—or of massive recourse to foreign immigration—which is no longer feasible in many countries because of the persistent economic stagnation and unemployment now affecting a large proportion of national workers. This combination of adverse factors cannot fail to raise doubts as to the very future of the social security schemes developed over the years in Europe, the level of which, in terms of the coverage provided and the population protected, is higher than it has ever been.

Protection against the contingency of old age, in other words the guaranteeing of an income to workers too old to continue participating in the production process, is one of the pillars of these schemes. It is based, sometimes implicitly but often explicitly, on what may be described as a "solidarity contract" between generations; those gainfully employed today contribute, from their wages or socialised production, enough to ensure that their elders can maintain a decent standard of living, in the hope or—until recently at least—in the conviction that they will be treated in the same way when it is their turn to stop working.

However, this solidarity contract is based upon an assumption which is simplicity itself: a system of this kind can succeed only so long as there is a sufficient number of contributors, i.e. members of the active population who can produce enough to provide for the needs of the "beneficiaries", the retired persons and pensioners.

Consequently, the combined effect of the rapid ageing of the population, the slowing down of economic growth in certain countries and the generally large deductions made from national incomes for social security coverage in Europe could not fail to provoke an in-depth discussion on the very future of retirement pensions. This book is the ILO's contribution to that debate.

In the health field, the increasing ageing of European populations is also giving rise to certain changes, and even the questioning of certain basic assumptions. Health care schemes—including those run within the framework of social security, of which there are many in Europe—are being confronted with two major challenges: the first, which is discussed more often but is perhaps not so worrying, at least in the long term, is the problem of how to cope with the excessive costs and structural changes required within the health system to meet the needs created by the increase in the proportion of older persons; the second, to which it is undoubtedly more pressing to find an appropriate solution for the future, is the problem of gauging if, how and to what extent health systems and European societies, faced with the chronological ageing of their populations, can slow down the corresponding physiological process in individuals so that they may retain the productive capacities required at least to maintain the level of material and social well-being, whether collective or individual, attained through years of effort.

Finally, there is another aspect that is vital for the demographic future of Europe and, consequently, for its economic and social future: there must be an understanding of the reasons why fertility rates or, to put it in less technical terms, births, have been declining so much in recent years. It is therefore relevant to have a good grasp of this almost universal phenomenon, in order to outline a family policy capable of reversing or, failing that, at least of slowing down this trend and determining the role that social security might and should play in this context.

These are basic questions and no country can, at the present time, dispute their validity.

The aim of the International Labour Office in publishing this study[1] is, then, to take stock of the present relationship between demographic developments and social security.

It begins by providing some statistical data regarding demographic changes in European countries, with emphasis on major population trends and inter-country variations (Chapter 1). The figures are taken from the latest available demographic studies and population projections, and the analysis takes into account not only the nature and possible future extent of the ageing process in the populations under study, but also expected developments with regard to the age groups covering children and young people. Clearly, it is extremely important to be able to estimate the needs of the younger generations and, if necessary, to re-examine the links between family policies and demographic developments in the light of these estimates.

The study continues with an analysis of the three separate aspects of the relationship between population changes and social security already mentioned in this introduction, namely:

(a) social security measures designed to support and strengthen the family, taking into account expected demographic changes;

(b) income maintenance for the elderly, in particular through pension schemes, taking into consideration the increasing number of pensioners in relation to the working population in employment;

(c) the increasing cost of medical care, resulting from the ageing of the population, financed by social security schemes.

Thus, Chapter 2 considers the role of social security benefits in family policies, on the basis of current demographic statistics and projections up to the year 2000. It first points out that changes in the age structure of populations in European countries have been accompanied by a radical change in traditional family structures and, above all, in family lifestyles. The family is less permanent and stable than it used to be and, with the number of children per family steadily declining (apart from a few rare exceptions), it is necessary to take a closer look at the very purposes of the family benefits granted by social security systems, either under the provisions of comprehensive legislation or through means-tested schemes.

In doing this, the study describes recent trends in Europe in this branch of social security, first noting that in most countries the share of family benefits in the total welfare budget is falling. It examines the reasons for this relative decline which, after all, has not come about by chance: it reflects either a change in the priorities assigned to the various functions of social security or a deliberate reaction on the part of governments and, in some cases, of employers' and workers' representatives when confronted with a particularly unfavourable economic situation. The study then points out that some legislations are moving towards greater selectivity in the granting of benefits, in that they target the subpopulations whose claims on resources would appear to be more clearly justified than those of other groups (deprived families, households under strain, etc.), although this trend is by no means universal.

Chapter 3 is first and foremost a reflection on the future of pension systems. In examining the prospects at country level, it endeavours to assess the weight to be accorded to the "demographic component" as one of the factors likely to have an impact on financing and on future trends in the cost of pension schemes—a subject which in many countries is arousing considerable misgiving. It then shows the ways in which the main countries under study plan to deal with the manifold problems posed by demographic changes when formulating their policies in favour of the elderly. It is clear that in some cases wide-reaching reform of national pension systems will be needed, reform which may prove successful or which may come up against sometimes insuperable obstacles. The situation in other countries, whose social security systems are based on legislative structures that are less vulnerable to the impact of the expected demographic developments, calls for a less sweeping approach: this is already under way in some countries. These analyses describe the manner in which governments are working to reconcile the sometimes diverging preferences of the social partners. They also attempt to show how much room for manoeuvre governments actually have, limited as they are, on the one hand, by the constraints of past policies and the rigidity of current systems and, on the other, by economic necessities which it would be a mistake to underestimate.

Using the background data already provided, and as a corollary to the study of policy options in the maintenance of old persons' incomes, Chapter 4 examines the problems encountered in providing health care for the elderly. These problems are, of course, by no means new, as regards either the effectiveness of care or the financial implications for health insurance schemes and national health services. Unfortunately, however, they are growing in gravity as longevity increases and the cost of medical treatment rises steadily—for obvious reasons. This chapter endeavours to assess the latest trends in the European countries which are particularly attentive to these problems. This has made it necessary, at the analytical stage, to go beyond the purely technical or financial aspects of the matter, in so far as the answers to the questions raised may depend on the position adopted by those who in their own countries are responsible for safeguarding the standards of medical ethics—or simply ethics in general.

Lastly, a brief conclusion sums up the main ways in which demographic constraints may in the coming years influence the development of systems of social protection in Europe. In so doing, it suggests broad guide-lines for possible further reflection on a subject which, without doubt, will remain one of the foremost concerns of social policy-makers and, of course, of the social partners.

In conclusion, it should be pointed out that it would not have been possible to complete the study without the invaluable assistance of such eminent European experts as:

— Mr. Paul Paillat, former Head of the Department of Social Demography, Institut national d'Etudes démographiques, France (population trends);
— Mr. David Piachaud, Professor in the Department of Social Science and Administration, London School of Economics and Political Science, United Kingdom (family policies);
— Mrs. Simone Sandier, Director of Research, Centre de Recherche, d'Etude et de Documentation en Économic de la Santé (CREDES), France (health care for the elderly).

The International Labour Office wishes to express its warmest thanks to all of them.

Note

[1] This study is an expanded version of ILO: *Demographic development and social security*, Report II, Fourth European Regional Conference, Geneva, September 1987.

POPULATION TRENDS IN EUROPE, 1985–2025

1

KEY FACTORS

The essence of demographic analysis has always been, and still is, to study the key factors in population processes: birth rates, death rates and migration. Nowadays, more work is being done on the structural effects of population change, both the purely demographic aspects (sex and age distribution) and the largely demographic aspects (the economically active or potentially active population; the already retired or the potentially retired, etc.).

At a given time, any population presents a structure which, by force of habit, is still referred to as a pyramid, even though it has long since lost all resemblance to the actual shape of a pyramid. The distribution on either side of a vertical axis of the total population classified according to age group (and possibly by other criteria such as marital status, nationality, economic activity, etc.) has the merits of simplicity and clarity: this should not, however, be allowed to mask the fact that it provides a static picture at a given point in time, whereas population is undergoing constant change as a result of fluctuations in birth rates (fertility), death rates (mortality) and migration. What is more, historical events (usually wars and their consequences) distort the structure to varying degrees and, as time passes, these distortions move up the age ladder, while changing in character.

For instance, the 1915–19 generations in countries depleted by deaths during the First World War tended to have fewer children than the more populous generations which came before and after them. Moreover, as these war-depleted groups age, they cause several fluctuations in the population structure: while there is a temporary downward trend in the number of retired persons (1975–2000), employment problems arise because larger generations, such as that of the economically prosperous years after the Second World War, arrive on the labour market. It is

7

unusual to find a country where the demographic curve is constant. Much of the social security system is affected by these irregularities in the population pyramid, and by their timing. This will be the main theme running through this study.

Which factors should be given priority when examining the repercussions of demographic development on social security systems? The answer is sex and age.

The *sex* factor should be examined first, for three major reasons:

1. There can be no reproduction, and therefore no population replacement, without women. The change in women's reproductive patterns affects the population's inherent and outward characteristics, since fertility, especially in Europe, is becoming increasingly a social phenomenon and no longer merely a random process.

2. The mortality and morbidity rates of women differ from those of men, particularly at both ends of the life span. These discrepancies make it necessary to undertake separate studies by sex and to use different calculations for life expectancy: the projections are, therefore, calculated according to sex, then combined to obtain the figures for the total population. Excess male mortality brings with it an increased risk of isolation for women, a factor which causes major problems in any social welfare programme for the elderly.

3. During the course of their working lives, men and women become entitled to the same rights; however, these differ in value for women, because most of them have had and still have an incomplete career and consequently receive a lower pension, at least in countries where the pension system in force is based mainly upon years of contribution.

Age is the next factor which must be taken into consideration.

However regrettable this may be, and however much one might envisage changing attitudes and regulations, the fact remains that age plays an often decisive and perhaps undue role in our societies. It restricts the granting of family allowances; it fixes the age at which we start and finish compulsory schooling; it delays entry into working life and, increasingly, determines the date of permanent withdrawal from the workforce (commonly known as "retirement"). Age is also a factor in the civil status of a population (minimum age at marriage), in its civic rights (voting age) and even in its legal status (the age of criminal responsibility may differ from that of civil liability).

From a demographic standpoint, two factors are geared to age: fertility and mortality.

As far as *fertility* is concerned, changes in the proportion of women of reproductive age have direct repercussions on the population process as a whole since, given a uniform reproductive pattern, the fewer the women, the fewer the children; moreover, the physiological capacity to bear children (fecundity) is not the same at all ages between 15 and 45.

Mortality, after the hazardous first year of life (infant mortality), is at a minimum between 5 and 15 years of age, before becoming more marked and finally accelerating after 50 years of age. This incidence has only to drop in certain periods of life and not in others, or among women rather than men, for the repercussions to be different. Thus, on the one hand, the spectacular fall in infant mortality (from birth to the child's first birthday) that has occurred over the past 30 years has limited the relative ageing of populations by increasing the proportion of children in the whole; on the other hand, a major decline in mortality after the ages of 50 or 60 would accelerate the ageing process by increasing the proportion of the elderly and the very old. *No group of the population is independent of the others.* This example shows how useful it is to calculate changing mortality rates in relation to an average or to other reference figures, such as those in the other sex, preceding age groups, other social classes, other environments (urban/rural) and so on. Such comparisons bring to light any cases of excess mortality or differential mortality.

The study of demographic development cannot therefore be limited to the sequence of rates of natural increase (balance of births and deaths) or of total increase (this balance, plus the balance of migration). The same applies to the assessment of future trends, because of chance fluctuations in the structure of the population. Of course, only one interpretation of these trends is given in this book.

It would be dangerous to believe that age groups are interchangeable. Some groups present such different characteristics that this might seem obvious; none the less, is not this type of error committed when it is thought that workers aged 60–64 years can be replaced by jobseekers of 20–24 years of age? Similarly, it would be misleading to put persons aged 85–89 years of age in the same category as those of 65–69 years of age, on the pretext that both groups belong to the "older population".

No population is homogeneous: any over-generalisation of the approach to demographic problems should, therefore, be avoided, the more so because people's needs differ, as do the institutions and resources available to meet those needs.

PROBLEMS RESULTING FROM DEMOGRAPHIC CHANGE

Having made these initial comments, we now examine the major aspects of demographic development in Europe (Europe as defined by the ILO), which are all the more significant because they affect the administration and financing of all the various branches of social protection, grouped under the generic term of social security.

From East to West and from North to South, a common feature is discernible, though it may be more pronounced in some places than in others: all the European populations are *ageing*, i.e. the proportion of elderly people is increasing, whether 60 or 65 years is taken to be the threshold of "statistical old age".

Given that the structure of the populations in question was fairly different in the 1950s, it is only normal that the proportion of elderly people should be dissimilar today. However, the convergence of trends is undeniable: there is a slowing down of the ageing process in countries which already have an old population (with more than 12 per cent of persons aged 65 years and over in 1985), while in countries with a young structure the process is speeding up.

This common feature is accompanied by a further characteristic: demographic growth is stationary or almost stationary, if not actually negative, as in the Federal Republic of Germany. Only countries with a very young population, of which Turkey is the best example, escape from this general rule. This "stabilisation" is itself the consequence of a drop in fertility so steep that the number of births is now not much greater that the number of deaths: in some cases, the latter even outnumber the former.

At this stage, the concept of demographic ageing assumes a further dimension. For a long time, only specialists were interested in following the increasing levels of ageing, expressed in terms of the proportion of elderly people in the total population. Apart from these specialists, some were tempted to minimise the importance of the phenomenon, as long as the level remained between 8 and 10 per cent. The same will no longer apply tomorrow, when this level reaches 20–22 per cent, or even 20–25 per cent; by that time (which is not so far distant for some countries), *the structure as a whole will be affected*, including—and this point should be stressed—the internal composition of the working-age population (20–59 or 20–64 years of age). In point of fact, the term "ageing" will no longer be appropriate; it will even be misleading, because it places too much stress on the higher part of a structure which is no longer a pyramid but is assuming the form of a pillar. The continuous decline in fertility has erased the base of the pyramid and the future decline in mortality after 50 years of age will fill out its top.

The European social security systems were set up about 40 years ago, taking into account the demographic structure prevailing at that time. One may wonder if they will operate in the same way with the structures one can expect to see in the next 40 years—or much sooner in countries where the above-mentioned process is already extremely advanced.

To set the stage for the discussion on possible replies to this question, we first describe and comment upon the present situation and probable development of the total population of countries in this part of the world. For convenience the countries are divided into eight groups:

1. The European Economic Community (EEC)[1]
2. Northern Europe
3. Alpine Europe
4. Adriatic Europe
5. Mediterranean island countries
6. Eastern Europe
7. USSR
8. Turkey.

In the second part of this chapter, attention will be focused on ageing within the main population groups (internal ageing).

SOURCES AND METHODOLOGY

The population statistics used in this chapter are taken mainly from two United Nations publications.[2]

Among the possible variants set out in the United Nations projections, the medium variant has been selected for two reasons; first, the authors considered it to be the most plausible and, second, it is the only one presented with all the required details (structure by sex and by quinquennial age groups), measured at five-year intervals.

Theoretically, it would have been possible to rely on data published nationally but, first, such data do not exist for all countries in the area under study and, second, the time ranges covered by them do not necessarily coincide, which is obviously an obstacle to comparative study. The considerable volume of work carried out by the United Nations Population Division has in fact come in for some criticism, mainly from observers who have detected errors or who do not agree with the hypotheses on which it is based. Some such cases will be referred to in this study, but the fact remains that the United Nations documents are irreplaceable, for several reasons:

— they provide, in concise form, a body of information on population structures by age and sex, measured at five-year intervals from 1950 to 2025, the dates coinciding in all cases;

— they contain information on numerous demographic indicators, in a medium variant (adopted here) as well as in low and high variants.

11

These last two variants indicate the lower and upper limits within which the populations under study are most likely to evolve;

— on condition that each single figure is not taken as infallible, the documents constitute an extremely useful tool for determining orders of magnitude (numbers and proportions), by showing the structural changes expected to result from the various hypotheses.

This source of information has been improving since it was first published in 1980, thanks to help from national statistical services which have been invited to make any corrections they consider necessary or useful.

As regards likely future developments, it should be remembered that *projections* are neither forecasts nor predictions. All the figures are a function of the hypotheses on which they are based, in particular those relating to age-specific fertility, and mortality by age and sex. The documents also make reference to the hypotheses adopted for the migration projections, which are presented in the form of migratory balances: for some countries this may be the weakest part, but it could hardly be otherwise in that net migratory movements depend on political and economic conditions which are still in the future.

In the text itself, reference is made to two classic demographic concepts: life expectancy at birth and the total fertility rate, which it is relevant to define here.

Life expectancy at birth (symbol e_0) is the average number of years a newborn child (of either sex) may be expected to live *if* the mortality rate of the period of observation does not change. The actual average life span of this generation will be very much longer than e_0 if the war against disease and death continues to be successfully waged. This indicator is independent of the structure by age. It does not have predictive value in itself.

It is in the countries where the expectation of life at birth is lowest (i.e. where the average life-span is shortest) that the greatest progress is to be expected and hoped for, mainly as a result of a drop in infant mortality (Portugal is a good example). In countries where life expectancy is longest, it will be difficult to make much more headway, in that the current levels reflect consistent and judicious use of the advantages of economic, scientific and technical progress and of the infrastructure provided by existing institutions and services. Here, social security has a vital part to play.

The total fertility rate (TFR) represents the average number of children (of either sex) that women of reproductive age will have if their reproductive behaviour does not change. It is therefore not a predictive indicator as such; it reflects the current fertility rate.

At the rate of 2.1 children per woman, generations are renewed (at least in Western and Northern Europe); below this rate, they are not. A population may, however, continue growing for a certain time with a TFR lower than 2.1, but this indicates that the population is likely to age if the TFR does not increase in the near future and over a fairly long period. Table 1 shows changes in this rate between 1965 and 1986 for most European countries.

A caveat is in order here concerning the weak impact of sporadic fluctuations. Major population trends are so slow to change that demographers have coined the expression "population inertia". Minor fluctations in indicators that do not last longer than two years are without significance: in fact, it would be abnormal if such fluctuations did not occur, given the irregularities in population structures. Suppose that in one of the countries under study there were to be a marked rise in fertility. It would be a very long time before this had any noticeable effect on the age structure even though, long before this happened, absolute population numbers would begin to differ from those appearing in earlier projections: this is because proportions and ratios are resistant to change (except in the case of migratory movements). As far as can be seen, a continuing ageing of European populations is a much more plausible hypothesis than an increase in the proportion of young people or even a halt to the ageing process.

PRESENT SITUATION AND PROBABLE DEVELOPMENTS, BY AREA

The first part of this section is essentially a statistical exercise based on the figures contained in tables A.1 and A.2, included in the statistical appendix to this volume.

Present situation (1975–85)

In 1985 there were about 541 million inhabitants in Europe (excluding the USSR), of whom 321 million (59.3 per cent) lived within the boundaries of the European Economic Community (EEC); this proportion, however, was even higher among those of 65 years of age or over (67 per cent).

Alongside Europe proper lies the USSR, whose most populous areas are, of course, situated in Europe, but whose eastern boundaries stretch as far as the Pacific Ocean. In 1979 there were just over 278 million people living in the USSR, one feature of this population being its comparative and no doubt temporary youthfulness—only 9.3 per cent were over the

Table 1. Total fertility rate (average number of children per woman), European countries, 1965–86

Country	1965	1970	1975	1980	1982	1983	1984	1985	1986
Austria	2.70	2.29	1.83	1.65	1.66	1.56	1.53	1.48	1.47e
Belgium	2.60	2.24	1.73	1.69	1.60p	1.56p	1.52e	1.49e	n.a.
Denmark	2.61	1.95	1.92	1.55	1.43	1.38	1.40	1.45	1.50e
Finland	2.47	1.83	1.68	1.63	1.71	1.74	1.70	1.65	1.63e
France	2.84	2.47	1.93	1.95	1.91	1.79	1.81	1.82	1.84p
Germany, Fed. Rep. of	2.51	1.99	1.45	1.45	1.41	1.33	1.29	1.28	1.36e
Iceland	3.71	2.79	2.65	2.48	2.26	2.24	2.08	1.93	n.a.
Ireland	4.03	3.87	3.41	3.23	2.95e	2.74e	2.54e	n.a.	n.a.
Luxembourg	2.41	1.96	1.63	1.51	1.49	1.45	n.a.	n.a.	n.a.
Netherlands	3.04	2.58	1.66	1.60	1.50	1.47	1.49	1.51	1.56e
Norway	2.93	2.50	1.98	1.72	1.71	1.66	1.66	1.66	1.63e
Sweden	2.42	1.92	1.77	1.68	1.62	1.61	1.66	1.73	1.79e
Switzerland	2.61	2.10	1.61	1.55	1.55	1.51	1.52	1.51	1.52e
United Kingdom:									
England and Wales	2.85	2.40	1.78	1.88	1.76	1.76	1.76	1.78	1.78e
Scotland	3.00	2.57	1.91	1.84	1.73	1.70	1.68	1.71	n.a.
Northern Ireland	n.a.	3.13	2.63	2.72	2.47	2.42p	2.35e	2.35e	n.a.
Greece	2.32	2.43	2.33	2.21	2.02	1.94	1.82	n.a.	n.a.
Italy	2.55	2.37	2.19	1.66	1.57	1.53e	1.50e	1.42e	n.a.
Portugal	3.07	2.62	2.57	2.22	2.07	1.95	1.89	1.71	1.61e
Spain	2.97	2.87	2.80	2.18	1.87p	1.72p	1.65p	n.a.	n.a.
Yugoslavia	2.71	2.29	2.27	2.13	2.13	n.a.	n.a.	n.a.	n.a.
Bulgaria	2.07	2.18	2.23	2.05	2.02	2.00	1.99	n.a.	n.a.
Czechoslovakia	2.37	2.07	2.44	2.16	2.10	2.07	2.07	2.07p	n.a.
German Dem. Rep.	2.48	2.19	1.54	1.94	1.86	1.79	1.74	1.74	n.a.
Hungary	1.82	1.98	2.35	1.91	1.78	1.75	1.74	1.83	1.83e
Poland	2.52	2.20	2.27	2.26	2.34	2.42	2.37	2.31	2.20e
Romania	1.91	2.89	2.60	2.43	2.17	2.00	n.a.	n.a.	n.a.
USSR	2.46	2.39	2.39	2.25	2.29	2.37	2.41	2.40	n.a.

n.a. = not available.
e: estimate; p: provisional.

Source: A. Monnier: "La conjoncture démographique: l'Europe et les pays développés d'outre-mer", in *Population* (Paris, Institut national d'études démographiques), Nos. 4–5, 1987.

age of 65 as against 12.3 per cent in Europe west of the Soviet Union's frontiers.

The EEC[3]

In such a widespread area as the EEC, which stretches from the North Sea to the Aegean, it would be pointless to seek common population features at all costs. Nevertheless, in spite of some differences of degree, it is easy to see that the structure of the populations of all its member countries has already aged (for example, more than 13 per cent of the inhabitants of the following countries are over 65: Belgium, Denmark, Federal Republic of Germany, Greece, Italy, Luxembourg, United Kingdom) and will continue to age. The only notable exceptions are Ireland (10.9 per cent) and Spain (11 per cent).

Future developments will depend on fertility and mortality levels, and also on the balance of migration.

With regard to the first of these factors, *fertility*, the EEC countries — except Ireland—all appear to be heading for a level of fertility which is too low to ensure the replacement of their populations.[4] In 1950 the picture was not so clear-cut, since the Netherlands had an index of 3.1 at that time, comparable to that of Portugal in 1965. Furthermore, it is in the Netherlands that the greatest decline in fertility has occurred (the index falling from 3.1 in 1950 to 1.5 in 1985). The Federal Republic of Germany has been at this level, the lowest in its entire history, for a long time now.

The second factor, *mortality*, is extremely uneven, in terms both of overall mortality and of infant mortality. The latter, for instance, varies between 8 per thousand (Denmark and the Netherlands) and 20 per thousand (Portugal). In 1950 it ranged from 24 per thousand in the Netherlands to 91 per thousand in Portugal: this shows the progress made in 35 years.

A more realistic picture of the impact of mortality rates on population is obtained by taking the expectation of life at birth (e_0), thereby eliminating the effects of age structure. In 1985 the range in the EEC countries was as follows:

Life expectancy at birth (in years)		Men	Women
Maximum	Netherlands	72.7	79.5
Minimum	Portugal	68.4	75.2

Inasmuch as there is at present a movement towards harmonisation—if not to actual unification—of the social security systems of EEC members, mortality rates can be expected to fall, offsetting in some small degree the narrowing of the base of the age pyramid, which depends more on fertility levels.

At present, external *migration* constitutes the major factor in measuring differences between the countries. It should not be forgotten that countries such as France and the Federal Republic of Germany were big importers of labour, whereas other countries, such as Portugal, Spain, Italy and Greece (not to mention countries outside the EEC), were big exporters—Portugal being the most striking example. Communication facilities and paid leave make it possible to offset to a great extent the adverse effects of the long-term emigration of young men and women on national fertility rates, and therefore on the demographic structure of the country of origin. For its part, the contribution of foreign workers, as permanent residents, to the fertility of the host country can be significant (this is the case of France, where one out of 14 children is born of non-national parents); however, this brings with it a social problem for which it is difficult to find a solution—that of integrating young people ("second-generation immigrants") into the host society.

Northern Europe

From west to east, Northern Europe includes four countries (Iceland, Norway, Sweden and Finland) which differ in several respects but have many cultural features in common. Iceland stands apart for two reasons: it is an island and is sparsely populated.

In this area, Sweden is a benchmark. It is the country in which fertility has declined the most[5] and, consequently, it also has the structure which has aged the most (already in 1975, 15.1 per cent of Swedes were 65 years of age and over). However, this is offset by the fact that, with its low mortality level, it has one of the highest life expectancy rates in the world (1980–85: men, 73.4; women, 79.4). It is therefore not surprising that Sweden should also have a social welfare system which is often held up as an example.

Although Norway and Sweden border upon each other, the contrast between them shows that it is not enough to be neighbours to be similar: in 1985 the proportion of elderly Norwegians was only 13.7 per cent.

For the time being, Finland is holding its own against the ageing process but, like the Scandinavian peninsula, it is very sparsely populated north of the 62nd parallel. Its geographical location, however, is such that it cannot be treated in the same way as Norway or Sweden. One feature of note is that in Finland the gap between male and female longevity is one of the widest in the world, comparable to that of its neighbour, the USSR, and that of France (just over eight years).

Although Denmark is a member of the EEC, it should not be forgotten that, both geographically and culturally, it is part of Scandinavia, with which it maintains particularly close relations. Its population characteristics are nearer to those of its Northern neighbours than to those of EEC countries bordering on the Mediterranean.

Alpine Europe

At the heart of geographical Europe, Austria, Liechtenstein and Switzerland constitute a continuous mountain strip.

In spite of its irregular relief, population density is often high in this area (Switzerland: 154 inhabitants/km^2). Ageing in Switzerland is taking place at more or less the same pace as in Austria (in 1985, the elderly population was 14 per cent and 14.1 per cent respectively). The two countries' TFRs are also very similar, but by 1970 this indicator had, in Switzerland, fallen below that of Austria with, however, a narrowing of the gap more recently: it is now one of the lowest in Europe. In Austria the rapid expansion of the capital has contributed in no small measure to ageing in the country as a whole, since Vienna, with its large population (1.5 million inhabitants), is also a city of the elderly (20.9 per cent in 1981).

Mortality rates still differ considerably between the two countries, recalling the contrast to be found in Scandinavia. Fertility levels and trends, however, are much more similar and far below the replacement rate.

Adriatic Europe

Only the requirements of presentation and their geographical proximity justify the pairing here of Yugoslavia and Albania. There can be no question of comparing them, even though a sizeable Albanian minority lives in southern Yugoslavia (Kosovo, Metohija).

Because of its spread and its mixture of ethnic groups and cultures, Yugoslavia offers a diversity of demographic features which vary widely from one republic to another. Taking the country as a whole, however, it can be seen that there is still progress to be made in the battle against mortality, as there is in Albania. Fertility in Yugoslavia is high enough to ensure the replacement of generations, although there is no comparison with that in Albania (TFR: 2.1 as against 3.6).

Furthermore, Yugoslavia has experienced large-scale migratory flows, especially towards the Federal Republic of Germany. It is clear that emigration has limited local unemployment, but it hardly provides a long-term solution, given the restrictive policies adopted by the host countries as a result of their own unemployment problems.

It is worth while noting the extreme "youthfulness" of the Albanian population, since this is a guarantee of rapid population growth.

Mediterranean island countries

Malta and Cyprus are both sovereign islands in the Mediterranean: this is their one common feature. They differ in other respects, if only in their population characteristics.

The ageing of the population is more marked in Cyprus than in Malta, whereas birth rates are higher. This is less of a paradox than it would appear to be, since both populations are small and Cyprus has experienced and is still experiencing a troubled period in its history.

Eastern Europe

Bulgaria, Czechoslovakia, the German Democratic Republic, Hungary, Poland and Romania are all part—*de facto* and *de jure*—of a single political and economic community: their economic and social systems are similar. Notwithstanding the common link binding these countries, their demographic features vary, because a country's history, culture and level of economic and social development help to maintain certain differences.

The German Democratic Republic differs from its partners in that it is the country with the oldest population (for a long time, its ageing rates were even the highest in the world); its fertility level is the lowest in the area, in spite of efforts made to encourage women to have children. This policy has nevertheless succeeded in maintaining fertility at a much higher level than in the Federal Republic of Germany and in checking the ageing process.

Whereas in the other countries of the area fertility is markedly higher than in the EEC countries (except Ireland), the expectation of life at birth is lower, particularly for Hungarian males and Romanian females. With their combination of relatively high fertility and relatively low mortality, Romania and, to a lesser degree, Poland possess a potential for population growth which will be discussed later in this chapter.

The USSR

The USSR is almost a continent in itself; the European part, although the most densely populated, covers the smallest area. There are considerable demographic differences inside the Soviet Union, especially as regards the size of the population in the constituent republics: figures range from 142 million inhabitants in the Russian Soviet Federal Socialist Republic (RSFSF) to 1.5 million in Estonia. However, the fact of belonging to the same political, economic and social entity makes up somewhat for this heterogeneity.

Nevertheless, there is a problem of statistical information. Thanks to the 1979 census, structural data for the USSR and its republics and regions are available, of which some are given later in this book; however, demographic factors are less well known. For purposes of consistency with the rest of the study, United Nations figures for 1985 are used. To illustrate the internal differences, reference is made to a United States study, which itself was drawn up on the basis of USSR sources (table 2).[6] A comparison of estimates for 1985 shows that the two documents tally to a large extent.

In terms of ageing, the small republic of Latvia closely resembles Western Europe and for the same major reason: its low fertility rate. It

Table 2. Population and age structure in the USSR and some of its constituent republics, 1979 and 1985

	USSR	RSFSR[1]	Ukrainian SSR	Byelorussian SSR	Latvia	Uzbekistan
1979 census						
Population (millions)	261.1	137.4	49.6	10.0	2.5	15.4
Estimated structure (%):						
0–19 years	34.2	30.7	29.8	32.0	28.1	53.4
60 and over	12.9	13.7	15.7	14.4	16.8	7.2
65 and over	11.1	10.0	11.1	10.3	13.1	5.4
1985 estimate						
Population (millions)	277.7[2]	142.0	51.2	10.1	2.5	18.2
Structure (%):						
0–19 years	32.4	28.5	28.3	30.4	26.3	51.6
60 and over	13.0	14.0	16.1	13.9	17.7	6.3
65 and over	9.2	10.0	11.4	9.7	12.7	4.4
TFR	2.2[3]	2.1	2.1	2.1	2.1	4.6

[1] Russian Soviet Federal Socialist Republic   [2] United Nations figure: 278.6.   [3] United Nations figure: 2.35.

Source: G. S. Baldwin: *Population projections by age and sex for the republics and major economic regions of the USSR, 1970 to 2000* (Washington, DC, United States Bureau of the Census, 1979).

differs considerably from the Asian republics, represented here by Uzbekistan; demographically speaking, their structure is that of developing countries. With a total fertility rate (TFR) of 4.6 (compared with 2.1 in the RSFSR), it is not surprising that considerably more than half of the population is under 20 years of age and that the population growth in these Asian republics is much more rapid than in the republics west of the Ural mountains.

The ratio of the economically inactive to the active population (the dependency ratio) therefore varies considerably (see Chapter 3). For instance, in the Ukrainian SSR the ratio

$$\frac{(0-19)+(60+)}{(20-59)}$$

was 79.8:100 (1985) compared with 141.3:100 in Uzbekistan (average for the Soviet Union: 83.0:100).

On the mortality side, the figures given in the *1985 Economic Yearbook (USSR)* make it possible to estimate expectation of life at birth for the whole of the Soviet Union as 64 years for men and 73 for women. According to the United Nations, the corresponding figures over the period 1980–85 would be 66.5 and 75.4; the gap between the two sexes is about the same, and is wider than in Western Europe.

Turkey

Turkey, with its large population (49 million in 1985) and surface area, and specific characteristics, warrants separate examination.

Both its higher TFR (4.0) and its low level of ageing (4.2 per cent) are in marked contrast to other European figures, even those of Ireland and Albania.

While there has, of course, been a drop in fertility, Turkey's demographic structure will long remain the youngest in this part of the world.

Probable developments (1985–2025)

By adopting the same distribution as in the previous section, the medium variant of the United Nations projections (1985) will allow the probable development of the population and its main components to be followed from 1985 to 2025, with an intermediary cut-off point at the year 2000. The 1985 estimates are taken as a basis (1985 = 100).

The EEC

A population growth rate of about 3 per cent over 40 years is expected in the EEC, although this growth will be extremely uneven. Whereas a sharp decline in the number of persons under 20 years of age (-14 per cent) is expected, the number of persons aged 65 years and over might, after the year 2000, soar and reach even higher figures than in 1985 (index: 149).

As regards actual numbers, it is expected that there will be an additional 9 million people between 1985 and 2000, followed by a fall of 1 million (2000–2025). These are the two major findings.

It is estimated that there will be 21 million additional older people between 1985 and 2025, with a marked upturn between 2000 and 2025 (more specifically between 2015 and 2025), as shown below.

Older persons (65 years and over)	1975	1985	2000	2015	2025	Increase 2025/1985
Number (in millions)	40.0	42.3	50.1	56.9	63.0	20.7
Index	95	100	118	135	149	

Having accounted for 74 per cent of the older population in the EEC in 1985, the nationals of France, the Federal Republic of Germany, Italy and the United Kingdom are alone still expected to account for 71 per cent in 2025. The slight falling off in their increase would make them lose some percentage points out of the EEC total, without undermining their influence to any great extent.

Women, who in 1985 made up almost 58 per cent of the total number of old persons, are expected to maintain this level in 2025: this stability reflects a delayed restoration of balance, brought about by the arrival in older age groups of generations which were less affected than others by the consequences of the First World War. In 2025 Belgium, Denmark, Portugal and the United Kingdom should have a higher proportion of older women than the average for the area. Some countries will be more affected than others: Portugal (60.6 per cent of elderly people who are women), the United Kingdom (58.5 per cent), Denmark (58.3 per cent) and Belgium (58.2 per cent). This is a sign of the profound effects of ageing which merits close attention.

Northern Europe

Total population numbers are expected to remain almost unchanged, dropping slightly from 17.6 million to 17.3 million; this is in spite of developments in Sweden, a country which might alone lose 644,000 inhabitants but which, above all, could record an increase in its older population: 293,000 more elderly people out of a total increase of 989,000 over the whole area.

Finland may no longer be a country with a relatively young population, as it was in 1985; it could well find itself among those with a much higher level of ageing in 2025 (21 per cent of older persons instead of 12.3 in 1985). At the same time, the numbers of young people under 20 may drop by an average of about 15 per cent (in Sweden, 23 per cent). More than half the population in the economically active age groups (54 per cent) could be over the age of 40, instead of 43 per cent in 1985.

Alpine Europe

Switzerland and Austria are expected to lose "only" 6 per cent of their populations from 1985 to 2025, i.e. 0.8 million, but this negative demographic growth is one of the signs of increased ageing: it is estimated that the proportion of older inhabitants will increase from 14 per cent in 1985 (already a high level) to 22 per cent in 2025, whereas the share of young people under 20 years of age will shrink considerably (-23 per cent).

Fertility levels, as projected in the medium variant, are sufficient to account for these developments (see table 1).

Adriatic Europe

Yugoslavia must expect an increase in its population, even if the growth rate slows down; it is estimated that it will have 3.6 million additional inhabitants in 40 years' time. The most surprising aspect of this trend is that it will be accompanied by an "explosion" of the older population (index: 243), which would put the country into the "aged" population category (17.3 per cent of old people in 2025).

Even more surprising could be the situation in Albania, since the index of population growth among elderly persons there is expected to reach 379, although the proportion will not exceed 10 per cent. This resistance to ageing is a good example of the impact of an initially young age structure and the effect of a high birth rate.

Mediterranean island countries

Although it should not experience very large-scale growth, Malta's population is nevertheless expected to increase from 383,000 to 549,000 (a growth index of 120), while its older population will more than double (index: 225). The fertility hypothesis adopted would lead to a drop in the proportion of young people under 20 years of age (from 31.3 per cent to 27.5 per cent, i.e. an index of 88).

The population of Cyprus is also expected to increase (index: 135), and this trend could be even more marked were the island at last to experience a more peaceful period in its existence: the "youthfulness" of the Turkish minority cannot but contribute to this growth. According to the United Nations projection, numbers in the 0–19 age group should decline slightly, but less so than in Malta (index: 85).

Eastern Europe

A population increase of 17 per cent over a 40-year period, as is expected in Eastern Europe, may seem modest in comparison with trends in the developing countries. It is nevertheless an astonishing rise in the European context, in sharp contrast to the very slight increase in the population of the EEC (+3 per cent). A sure sign is that the number of young people under the age of 20, instead of declining, is expected to remain stable; although a slight falling-off in figures for those under 5 years of age might herald a drop in the level, this movement is not sufficiently pronounced to be considered separately from the hypotheses put forward by the United Nations demographers.

Romania is expected to record the highest increase in young people (index: 167), in marked contrast to the German Democratic Republic (index: 100) or Hungary (index: 99), while it is calculated that the level of young people in Bulgaria and Poland will stabilise (index: 101).

The sharp increase in the number of older people (index: 183 for the area as a whole) confirms that ageing will be the outstanding feature of the twenty-first century: its level is expected to attain 16.6 per cent, compared with 10.6 per cent in 1985. However, this movement is likely to be very uneven, as can be seen by examining the 2025 data, country by country.

	Country						Eastern Europe
	Bulgaria	Czecho-slovakia	German Democratic Republic	Hungary	Poland	Romania	
% 65 and over (2025)	16.7	16.2	18.0	19.0	17.1	14.5	16.6

The range between the German Democratic Republic and Romania is extremely wide; in the low variant the gap between the two countries would remain unchanged. For it to disappear, the German Democratic Republic would have to follow the high variant (with a TFR of 2.7) and Romania the low variant (TFR: 2.0): this is hardly likely to happen.

The USSR

This vast country will become even larger—in terms of its population size—since the increase is expected to be 32 per cent, with the total population exceeding 368 million by 2025, i.e. 39 million more than in the EEC at that date.

Of even greater interest are the structural changes within this population. For instance, the proportion of young people under 20 years of age, which was 32.1 per cent in 1985, is expected to fall to 29.3 per cent, representing a decline in contrast to average trends; this is largely due to the lower growth rates of the very young (0–4 years), for which the index is likely to be 125; in 2025, however, it is projected, with the medium variant, that the TFR will remain well above the level required to ensure the replacement of generations (2.25 instead of 2.35 in 1985). This is a further example of the slow process of structural change (which the demographers call "population inertia"), implying that long periods of observation are required before any pronouncements can be made on the lasting effects of changes.

It is precisely in the case of the USSR that the marked population growth is expected to prevent the percentage of older inhabitants from rising too much: it is calculated that the level in 2025 will be much lower than that of the EEC, 14.8 per cent as opposed to 19.1 per cent. According to the low variant, the elderly population would in any case not exceed 15.2 per cent (as in the United Kingdom in 1985).

Admittedly, this is not a level to be taken lightly, but it will not put as much pressure on the social security system as the levels in Western Europe.

Turkey

When examining the figures for 1985 in Turkey, with its very high level of fertility (TFR: 4.0) and high proportion of young people (0–19 years: 47.3 per cent), it can be expected, even with the medium variant, that there will be considerable growth in total population between 1985 and 2025: the index might reach 187 (representing 42.6 million additional inhabitants, i.e. slightly less than the total projected Spanish or Polish populations in 2025).

The fact that the population of young people under 20 years of age is expected to grow by "only" 32 per cent (which nevertheless would represent an increase of 7.5 million inhabitants) would seem to point to a probable falling off in figures, but this would only be really noticeable half-way through the twenty-first century. Meanwhile, the explosion among the older members of the population (aged 65 and over) is striking:

	1985	2000	2025	Increase (%)
Number (millions)	2.1	3.6	7.2	5.6
Percentage	4.2	5.5	8.4	

Even if the very old (80 years and over) still represent a minute proportion of the population (1 per cent of the total), the fact remains that, from 260,000 in 1985, they may well increase to 1,043,000 over the next 40 years, implying a growth index of 401.

THE INTERNAL AGEING PROCESS: EXAMINATION OF STRUCTURAL DISTORTIONS

In trying to determine reasons for the internal ageing process, it is not enough to examine total population dynamics, past and future, even paying attention to the older age group, because two outwardly similar movements may conceal internal changes; hence the need not to dissociate numbers and proportions. Several examples will be given of the discrepancy between the way these two indicators evolve. One such example may be observed when the increase in a segment of the population conceals its decline in the percentage of the total, merely because the other segments have been growing more rapidly.

Taking into account the sectors in which social security operates, it appears necessary, in the second part of this chapter, to examine the situation group by group (using the index: $1985 = 100$), in order to identify the structural changes, not to say distortions, whether in the case of beneficiaries of social security or of those who finance it. By proceeding in this way, the temptation to adopt an overall approach, which could in this field result in serious over-simplification, will be avoided.

Young people (0–19 years)

This heading in fact covers three subgroups: very young, pre-school children (0–4 years), children of school age (5–14 years), and adolescents (15–19 years), this last group spanning the transition between study and work. In practice, at country level these distinctions require some revision and refinement, for instance by adopting a higher entry age for compulsory schooling or the onset of adolescence. The important thing here is to note the respective changes in the aggregates for the subgroups listed above, taking care not to isolate them completely one from another and not to regard statistical thresholds as impermeable frontiers. Table A.3 in the statistical appendix provides a summary of the basic data, showing changes in absolute numbers within the three subgroups.

The very young (0–4 years)

It is in this subgroup that future developments are most difficult to foresee. The number (and proportion in the total population) of children in this age group depends on the soundness of the hypotheses adopted concerning fertility rates during the early years of the twenty-first century; the fact is that it is difficult enough to forecast the number of births even five or ten years ahead. It would seem that the United Nations demographers have been somewhat optimistic in their projections for this age group. We shall come back later to the numbers and percentages given in the low variant which, unfortunately, is not dealt with in as much detail as the other variants in the publications on which this chapter is based.

Subject to these reservations, what developments can be expected in the main areas of Europe between 1985 and 2025?

The EEC

In the EEC as a whole there should, in 2025, be 0.5 million fewer children aged 0–4 years than in 1985, after a levelling off between 1985 and 2000. This 3 per cent fall may seem very slight when spread over 40 years; but the down-trend will not necessarily end in 2025, which is merely a reference point on the time-scale. Denmark (index: 79) is expected to be the most seriously affected by this drop in numbers, whereas Spain should gain 7 per cent (202,000 children) if the medium variant turns out to be correct—which is rather doubtful given the fertility trends in that country. The same applies to Italy.

Northern Europe

The decline should be even steeper in Northern Europe, since the index may fall as low as 89, though the movement will be spread more evenly than in the EEC countries.

Alpine Europe

With an index of 86, the decline should be greater in this area than in the preceding two.

Adriatic Europe

In Adriatic Europe numbers are expected to remain fairly stable thanks, as one might say, to an increase in the 0–4 age group in Albania: the Albanian figures should rise from 382,000 in 1985 to 500,000 in 2025, offsetting a decline in the corresponding figures for Yugoslavia—in spite of the disparity of the two population sizes.

Mediterranean island countries

In Malta and Cyprus the very young should just about hold their own (indices: 91 and 95 respectively); this would result in a perceptible fall in their share in the total population (to 6.3 per cent and 7.0 per cent).

Eastern Europe

One can speak of stability in this part of Europe after, however, a slight decline in 2015. Poland (index: 91) and, to a lesser extent, Hungary (index: 96) could push down the numbers, were it not for the demographic vigour of Romania and Czechoslovakia (indices: 112 and 106).

The USSR

The Soviet Union is expected in 40 years' time to have 11 per cent more young children than in 1985, an increase of 2.2 million—more than the total number of Romanian 0–4 year-olds at that time.

Turkey

Here there can be no illusions. To be sure, there should be 160,000 more very young Turks by 2025 (index: 125), but even this increase would not prevent their share in the total population from falling from 13 per cent in 1985 to 9 per cent in 2025.

School-age children (5–14 years)

These young people will only be present from 2000 onwards, since even the oldest among them were not yet born in 1985: this is even more obviously the case for the youngest of them. If we take the year 2025, most of the mothers of these children will not even have been born in 1985.

The EEC

To lose, as could the EEC countries, 5.4 million school-age children or, to be more precise, for the registers to decline by this number by 2025, would mean a steeper drop than in the younger age group. This difference results in part from the fertility assumptions adopted in the projections (the TFR in 2000 ranging from 1.4 for Denmark to 2.5 for Ireland). It is not impossible that in some countries the predicted fertility rates may be too high in comparison with the most plausible figures for that date (in Spain, for example, and in the Federal Republic of Germany).

Northern Europe

Sweden's index (76) of school-age children by the year 2025 is expected to be higher than that of Denmark (65), but much lower than the average for the whole area (81). It will reflect a downward trend in the number of young children between 1985 and 2000, leading to a fall in the number of 5–14 year-olds between 2000 and 2015.

Alpine Europe

In Switzerland there should be a marked decline, with the index falling to 75. In Austria the index should not go below 89.

Adriatic Europe

As far as population is concerned, Yugoslavia (index: 89) should develop on a par with the EEC countries, but Albania will be in a completely different situation, with a steeply rising index (134), out of all proportion to that of the other European countries, Turkey excepted.

Mediterranean island countries

The situation in Malta is expected to remain stable, whereas there should be a rise in Cyprus (index: 124).

Eastern Europe

Some degree of homogeneity is forecast in this area of Europe, with a range of indices (from 82 to 107) which is narrower than in the EEC countries (65–107).

The USSR

The growth index for the 5–14 year-old subgroup (122) is expected to be higher than that of younger children (index: 109), but lower than that for the population as a whole (index: 132). This will mark the beginning of stabilisation only if the reality confirms the projections.

Turkey

The steep rise in the school-age population (index: 134) masks a drop in its share of the total: it is expected that the proportion of 5–14 year-olds will fall from 23.4 per cent in 1985 to 16.8 per cent in 2025. A similar situation has already been noted in connection with the younger age group (0–4 years).

Adolescents (15–19 years)

In industrialised societies, adolescence is a new juncture in a person's existence, in that it brings with it increased awareness of the meaning of working and political life. It is important for the transition to be successful if adolescents are to become a dynamic force in tomorrow's society. It is also a period of uncertainty: young people hesitate to take the plunge into working life unless they have to, and often get off to a poor start if they are forced into it. This makes adolescence a crucial time of life to which the whole of society should pay more attention, in particular by putting more, and more judicious, effort into schooling and vocational training.

The size of this age group will shrink considerably, especially in Northern Europe and in the Alpine countries where, compared with 1985, one-third of its numbers will be absent from the 2025 roll-call.

The EEC

In 2025 the number of adolescents in the EEC countries is expected to be 18.9 million compared with 25.7 million in 1985—a drop of 6.8 million. This drop is greater than that forecast for school-age children (−5.4 million), even though the latter group covers a ten-year age span. The Netherlands and Denmark will lead the decline, with indices as low as 59. In Italy the fall in numbers may be all the more spectacular in that it will affect a large country and could amount to some 30 per cent (i.e. −1.7 million).

Northern and Alpine Europe

The projections point to a major decrease in the number of adolescents, with the index falling to 71; in Sweden it could even be as low as 68.

The decline should be similar, though a little steeper, in the Alpine countries (index: 63), especially in Switzerland (index: 58).

The rest of Europe

The situation will be quite different in Adriatic Europe and the island countries, in Eastern Europe and in Turkey.

Eastern Europe, for instance, presents a striking contrast, with the number of adolescents expected to rise by 7 per cent (representing an additional 545,000). This is a far remove from the trend in the EEC countries, which are expected to lose an average of 26 per cent (index: 74) of this age group. Even Ireland, with an index of 111, should lag far behind Poland (index: 120).

The slight slowing down of population growth in Turkey would still mean an increase of one-third in the number of adolescents over the 40 years under study (index: 136).

The USSR

The USSR is expected to have to make provision for 6.4 million additional adolescents by 2025. Their growth index (132) should be equal to that of the total population, but much higher than that of the very young (109).

Young people as a whole (0–19 years)

Overall, the EEC countries are expected to have 12.7 million fewer young people in 2025 than in 1985, a decline of 14.2 per cent, whereas in Eastern Europe the numbers should remain more or less stable.

From a structural point of view, a calculation of the share of each subgroup in the total number of young people reveals in both areas (and in the USSR) a change in the proportions. Thus, in the EEC the 1985 percentages for each of the subgroups were 22.6—48.7—28.7; in 2025 it is thought that they will be 25.6—49.8—24.6. In Eastern Europe the two sets of figures should be: 25.7—50.9—23.4 (1985) and 25.3—49.7—25.0 (2025). The similarity between the percentages is striking; however, this situation will arise only if there is a slight increase in fertility rates in the EEC countries.

Alongside this decline, on the one hand, and stability, on the other, the number of young people in the USSR should rise by one-fifth (index: 120.7) with, however, some signs of a slowing down, much more marked in the case of the very young, for whom the 2025 index is expected to be only 111. But before speaking of an "ageing" of the younger population, it is relevant to examine the changes in the internal structure of this group: for the USSR, the above-mentioned series would be: 28.0—49.4—22.6 (1985) and 25.2—50.1—24.7 (2025). The similarity is again obvious. In spite of the initial differences, these figures point to a convergence in demographic structures, but this remains to be confirmed by the facts.

*

* *

It is this very large group (0–19 year-olds) which will progressively become the driving force of the Europe of the twenty-first century, but it will only succeed if its qualities and skills enable it to do so.

Mention must be made here of the part expected to be played by lower fertility levels. Any decline in the percentage of young people in total population will automatically result in an increased percentage of old people, but the institutions, services and human and other resources provided for them are not interchangeable. Nor can the longer-term implications be ignored: not only will populations be "older", but they will also be smaller in number.

The working-age population (20–59 years)

In the present (and perhaps temporary) circumstances, the working population is for the most part made up of men and women aged between 20 and 59. The age groups in question are, as it were, the source from which the economy draws its strength.

There is too great a difference between a young man or woman of 20 years of age and a 50 year-old for one not to be tempted to divide this wealth of human resources, in demographic terms, into two halves. The first covers all those aged 20–39 years, who are starting out on their working life and improving their skills; the second includes those aged 40–59 years, who have gained experience and, in any case, length of service. The overall distortion of the population structure will result in a transfer of persons from the first to the second on such a scale that sometimes the latter will outnumber the former by the year 2025. Opinions vary as to the effect of this structural distortion, but it is universally acknowledged that it is a phenomenon unprecedented in history. Table A.4 in the statistical appendix summarises the situation in European countries.

The fluctuations in the index numbers in table A.4 reflect fluctuations in the absolute numbers in the age groups in question. Any upward or downward departure from "normal" population trends (governed by current mortality) will be felt right up until the death of the last remaining survivors of this "accident of history". Good examples of this are the depleted age groups in the countries seriously affected by the First World War (a deficit of births), and "baby-boom"generations of 1946–65, which were flanked on both sides by periods of low fertility. It is not, then, surprising that for some years the 40–59 age group will outnumber the 20–39 age group. Thus it is also to some extent "normal" that such a situation should arise in 2025, since the population groups which will at that time be in the 20–39 age group (i.e. born between 1986 and 2005) are likely to be considerably smaller in size than those born between 1966 and 1985. Grouping populations by area tends to blur somewhat these fluctuations.

The EEC

In the EEC the group of potentially active young people (20–39 years) is expected to decline by 15.1 million between 1985 and 2025. This is as if the total population of the Netherlands in 1985 were to disappear.

During the same period, the older group (40–59 years) should increase by 9.3 million, with the result that the ratio of the 40–59 group to the 20–39 group should reach 107:100, after having peaked at 117:100 in 2015, whereas in 1985 it was still only 80:100.

Throughout the same period, and on the basis of the same hypotheses concerning mortality, there will be changes in the internal balance within the large working-age group (20–59 years), subdivided into eight five-year age groups. In the EEC as a whole in 1985 the 40–59 subgroup represented 44 per cent of the 20–59 group; in 2000 it is estimated that this figure will be 48 per cent, before reaching 51 per cent in 2025. In other words, the older group will slightly outnumber the younger one.

These changes will probably be felt most keenly by the Netherlands, because the ratio of the age group 40–59 to the age group 20–39 is expected practically to double in 40 years, increasing from 66:100 to 123:100, i.e. an even greater change than in Denmark (from 77:100 to 122:100).

Northern Europe

It is predicted that developments will be similar to those described for the previous area; however, they will be more marked because the index of the younger group should drop to 75 (a loss of 25 per cent), whereas, in the older group, it will increase to 118. Consequently, the ratio between the two groups will be close to 117:100 in 2025. The age group 55–59 and the age group 20–24 may be compared to show to what extent the generations concerned will fail to be replaced. The ratio is expected to develop as follows:

	1985	2000	2015	2035
Ratio $\dfrac{55-59}{20-24}$	77	99	118	131

Sweden will lead the way in this area: its own ratio will increase from 75:100 to 137:100.

Alpine Europe

The highest rates in this respect would seem to be in Switzerland, with a ratio of the age group 40–59 to the age group 20–39 reaching 123:100, a figure comparable to that of the Netherlands. In Austria the ratio will be 112:100.

Adriatic Europe

The working-age population in Yugoslavia should undergo ageing to a certain extent; the ratio of the older to the younger group is expected to reach 103:100 in 2025, whereas it will remain far below 100 in Albania (79).

Mediterranean island countries

In spite of a slight decline in Malta and Cyprus in the year 2000, the corresponding figures for these two countries should remain below 100 in the year 2025 (97 and 90).

Eastern Europe

The figures for Eastern Europe reveal the extent to which the initial situation plays a role in projected trends. It is expected that, after a steep rise in 1985, the ratio of the age group 40–59 to the age group 20–39 will tend to stabilise at 98:100, because the younger group, whose index will remain close to 100, will continue to hold its ground. The German Democratic Republic and Hungary might not experience such favourable conditions (indices 89 and 85, compared with 124 in Romania).

The USSR

The figures for the 20–59 age group are so impressive (more than 152 million in 1985 and 184 million in 2025) that the possibility of internal changes is not immediately apparent. It is nevertheless worth examining whether there might not be any. In 1985 the ratio of the 40–59 age group to the 20–39 age group was 76:100, demonstrating a relatively young structure; in 2025 it is expected to be 87:100, i.e. representing an increase so slight that it can be used for predicting developments only after the period under examination.

Turkey

For many years ahead, Turkey will be spared the ageing of its working-age population, since in 2025 the 40–59 age group is expected to represent only 79 per cent of the 20–39 age group, in spite of a marked increase since 1985: the index for the older group (274) will far exceed that of the younger one (185), but it should not be forgotten that in 1985, the ratio of the older to the younger group was only 54:100.

*
*   *

The crucial, underlying question is the following: Will an ageing active population be able to remain as dynamic, creative and adaptable as a younger active population with the same technical know-how? If the reply is negative or even doubtful, it is vital that ways be sought of countering this danger.

Older persons (65 years and over)

Internal trends

The reason for setting the statistical threshold here at 65 years of age is that the 60–64 age group is in an ambiguous situation, not least because of the falling activity rates after 60 years of age. All socio-gerontological research has shown that there is not *one* old population but *several*.

To avoid over-complicating the situation, the group of so-called "old people" will be divided into only two subgroups: those of 65–79 years of age and those of 80 years of age and over, with no attempt to oppose an "old" to a "very old" population, which places too much emphasis on chronological ageing alone. The advantage of proceeding in this manner is that it brings out the "ageing" of the oldest section of the population, the group which requires the most care. Table A.5 in the statistical appendix summarises the basic data concerning trends in these age subgroups, country by country, while figure 1 shows the proportion of persons over 64 years of age in European countries in 2015.

The EEC

In the EEC the average ratio of the age group 80 and over to the age group 65–79 was 27:100 in 1985, with a very wide internal range, varying from 17:100 in Portugal to 34.8:100 in France. In 2025 the average ratio is expected to remain much the same, but the gap between countries should narrow a little, ranging from 21:100 in Portugal to 31.2:100 in the Federal Republic of Germany. There is likely to be a reshaping of situations, because some will become stable and others worsen or improve. France is expected to be in this latter category, since its ratio is predicted to drop from 34.8:100 to 23:100. This will reflect the country's former demographic situation: in the year 2025, the 80 and over age

Figure 1. Proportion of persons over 64 years of age in European countries, 2015

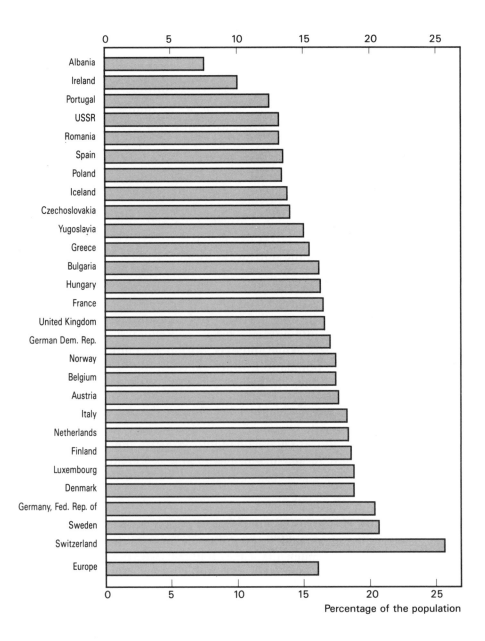

Percentage of the population

Source: United Nations: *World population prospects. Estimates and projections as assessed in 1982*, Population Studies, No. 86 (New York, 1986).

35

group will have been born before 1945, which also means that this future ratio can only be temporary. Projections need only to be extended beyond 2025 to measure to what extent the excessive ageing process will be resumed.

Northern Europe

In Northern Europe the 65–79 age group is expected to increase by one-third over the 40-year period, whereas the 80 and over age group should increase by almost a half, because of the influence of Finland. Undoubtedly, trends in Iceland are astonishing (for example, the index for 65–79 year-olds is expected to reach 221 in 2025 compared with 1985), but the population of this country is too small to change the average for the area.

Alpine Europe

Here the movement should be a little less marked, although the Swiss growth index for the 80 and over age group is nevertheless expected to reach 165, with the result that the ratio of this age group to the age group 65–79 would reach 31 : 100 (Austria: 28 : 100 after a temporary decline in the year 2000).

Adriatic Europe

Albania is a small country in terms of population size, and its demographic structure is remarkably young for a country situated in "old" Europe: paradoxically, however, if increasing numbers only are taken into account, it should beat all the ageing records. Thus, the 65–79 age group is expected almost to quadruple, while the 80 and over age group should more than quadruple. Nevertheless, the overall population structure should remain young in 2025, with the percentage of persons of 65 years and older still less than one-tenth (9.8 per cent) of the total population. The 80 and over age group should represent only 1.5 per cent, compared with 5.2 per cent in Sweden, for instance.

Mediterranean island countries

The predicted increase in the number of people aged 65 and over is striking, since the indices should more than double; but the structure as such should not change much. It is true that the scale is small, but that does not mean that at local level the problems will be any easier to resolve.

Eastern Europe

In Eastern Europe the almost identical growth of both age groups is a coincidence, in that developments are expected to be very different from country to country. In the German Democratic Republic the indices should be 87 for the 65–79 age group and 131 for the 80 and over age group by the year 2025, whereas in Romania they will probably be 191 and 228, thereby revealing an internal ageing of the older population, as in Bulgaria (156 and 208) and in Hungary (149 and 163). It is calculated that the average ratio of the older to the younger age group for this area will, therefore, be 24:100 (as against 23.5:100 in 1985).

The USSR

In the USSR it is predicted that there will be a much more rapid increase in the group of very old persons than in the 65–79 age group (indices: 216 and 175). In any case, these indices are high compared with those of the EEC or Northern Europe, areas which are at present the "oldest" in Europe. It may be assumed that in the long term the situations in the USSR and the EEC will converge; however, this will only happen after the year 2025 if, meanwhile, there is a marked drop in the fertility rate throughout the USSR (and not only west of the Urals), and if that in the EEC becomes stable.

Turkey

In 2025 Turkey should remain "young" since the percentage of old persons (65 years and over) is not expected to exceed 8.4 per cent of the total population. Nevertheless, judging by the increase in their ranks, it is obvious that the presence of 5.6 million more older Turks than in 1985 could create serious problems for the public authorities, both national and local, especially since it is estimated that the "very old" (80 years and over) will number more than 1 million, i.e. an almost fourfold increase over a period of 40 years.

Developments in the 80 and over age group

The numerical increase in the oldest group of the population in countries where overall demographic growth is expected to be very low (if not actually at zero) is, in itself, worthy of attention. It is expected that the EEC will have a further 4.3 million persons in this category in 40 years' time. Table 3 shows the situation, country by country, between 1985 and 2025. It may be seen that there is a wide variation in indices (United Kingdom: 128; Portugal: 215); this may indicate a convergence since the numbers of the very old are growing much faster in some countries than in others.

Even if, from now until 2025, a greater decline in mortality rates than that given in these projections can be expected, the fact that the upward trend will be more pronounced after 2015 and that it will not fall off

Table 3. Number of persons over 80 years of age in the EEC countries, 1985–2025 (in thousands)

Country	Year			Increase, 1985–2025	
	1985	2000	2025	Numbers	Indices (1985 = 100)
Belgium	287	296	387	100	135
Denmark	162	195	235	73	145
France	1 741	1 502	2 111	370	121
Germany, Fed. Rep. of	1 951	1 980	2 855	904	146
Greece	261	325	457	196	175
Ireland	65	80	101	36	155
Italy	1 438	1 703	2 405	967	167
Luxembourg	8	9	14	6	175
Netherlands	347	423	614	267	177
Portugal	156	217	336	180	215
Spain	730	1 027	1 491	761	204
United Kingdom	1 732	2 011	2 211	479	128
EEC	8 878	9 763	13 217	4 339	149

Source: United Nations: *Global estimates and projections by sex and age: The 1984 assessment* (New York, 1987).

before 2045 (when the less numerous generations born after 1965 enter this age group) is already striking. In 2025 the total number of 80 year-olds and their elders might almost equal the total population of the Netherlands in 1985 (14.5 million).

The situation will be particularly acute in the Federal Republic of Germany and Italy, as both countries will have to deal with an extra 1 million or so persons in this group. Measured in indices, this increase will exceed 200 in Portugal (215) and in Spain (204), much higher than in the Netherlands (177). These indices show the extent of the problem with which the administrations of these countries will have to cope. In countries where, today, the proportion of these old people is already very high, equipment and services are known to fall far short of needs, themselves assessed at a minimum.

None of these situations anticipated for 2025 would have been evident in 1985 except to demographers carrying out in-depth studies of generations reaching 80 years of age after the year 2015.

Table 4. Proportion of persons over 80 years of age in the total population, 1985 and 2025, by area

Area	1985 (%)	2025 (%)	2025/1985
EEC	2.6	4.1	158
Northern Europe	2.9	4.6	159
Alpine Europe	3.2	5.6	175
Adriatic Europe	1.3	3.0	231
Mediterranean island countries	1.5	2.6	173
Eastern Europe	2.0	3.1	155
USSR	1.7	2.7	159
Turkey	0.5	1.1	220

Source: United Nations: *Global estimates and projections. . .* , op. cit.

The fact that the percentages of people aged 80 and over will still be extremely small in the year 2025 (table 4) should not be allowed to obscure the considerable increase in absolute numbers, as shown in table 3.

Notes

[1] Membership of the Community takes precedence over geographical location. Thus, Denmark is a Northern European country and Greece an Adriatic European country, as well as being members of the EEC.

[2] *World population prospects: Estimations and projections as assessed in 1984*, Population Studies, No. 98 (New York, 1986); *Global estimates and projections of population by sex and age: The 1984 assessment* (New York, 1987).

[3] Belgium, Denmark, France, Federal Republic of Germany, Greece, Ireland, Italy, Luxembourg, Netherlands, Portugal, Spain, United Kingdom.

[4] In 1970 the average number of children per woman was still 2.8 in Italy, 2.4 in Greece, 2.6 in Portugal and 2.9 in Spain. In 1984/85 the figures had fallen to 1.4, 1.8, 1.7 and 1.65 respectively (see table 1).

[5] Recently, Swedish birth rates have shown signs of recovery: it remains to be seen, however, whether this is just a passing phenomenon or heralds a more lasting trend.

[6] G. S. Baldwin: *Population projections by age and sex for the republics and major economic regions of the USSR, 1970 to 2000* (Washington, DC, United States Bureau of the Census, 1979).

SOCIAL SECURITY MEASURES DESIGNED TO SUPPORT AND STRENGTHEN THE FAMILY

2

This chapter examines developments in family policy in relation to demographic developments in Europe. Family policy is here confined to policies affecting families which have—or are likely to have—children. The focus is principally on recent changes, and the social security aspects of family policy are given greatest attention.

The goals of family policy, and the various forms it takes, are first analysed, before evidence on demographic developments is recalled. The context and the nature of developments in family policy are then reviewed considering, in turn, cash family benefits, child-care policies and parental support. Finally, the effects of these policies on demographic development are discussed, and some issues for the future are analysed.

THE OBJECTIVES OF FAMILY POLICY

"Family policy" is a term which has different meanings in different countries. In some it is considered to be primarily a matter of social security, while in others it is much more broadly conceived. Before considering demographic and family policy developments, it is therefore necessary to clarify the nature and goals of family policy.

Family policies can be defined as practical measures which focus on, or affect, the family unit and its members. Usually the underlying aim will be to improve the well-being and to strengthen the functioning of the family. Family policies may be seen as alleviating problems which beset families and, in sum, as directed at meeting family needs.

Family policies can be classified in a number of ways, one of which is the following:[1]

(a) countries with an explicit, comprehensive family policy—such as Czechoslovakia, France, Hungary, Norway and Sweden;

41

(b) countries with an explicit but narrowly focused family policy—such as Austria, Denmark, Finland, the Federal Republic of Germany and Poland;

(c) countries without any explicit family policy—such as the United Kingdom (as well as the United States and Canada).

All European countries, whether or not they have an explicit family policy, have a range of policies that affect families with children. These policies may be broadly distinguished in terms of their motives and objectives. At present there seem to be four main types of objective which may of course coexist in the same country.

First, there is family policy as population policy: this is reflected in the argument that the reduction of the birth rate is a threat to the national well-being of the country concerned. This was for a long time the view in France.

Second, there is the goal of protecting children, particularly those in the poorest families, from material deprivation and of redistributing income towards those with children. This approach was retained in Ireland when the 1984 Bill on income supplements for low-income families came into effect.

Third, there is the more recent concern with enabling families to make choices—a more neutral motivation than the first, designed to support all kinds of families. Sweden is an example of this approach.

Fourth, there is the harnessing of family policy to goals concerned with sex roles and the labour market. These may be of opposing intent. On the one hand, the aim may be to draw women into the labour market, as in Eastern Europe. On the other hand, the objective may be to enable women to stay out of the labour market as, for example, with benefits for one-parent families in the United Kingdom.

Historically, many countries have at various times emphasised some or all of these objectives. Indeed, the number of different, and sometimes irreconcilable, goals is an important characteristic of family policies which distinguishes them from other social security policies: they can be—and are—actively used to shape societies in different ways and directions. What perhaps all countries have in common, however, is the view that the family is the central institution for the birth, the care, the socialising and the economic support of children.

In addition to the common themes, there have in the past been more specific ones in many European countries, where family policies have been used as policy instruments to solve other national problems or support national ideologies. In the Federal Republic of Germany, for example, there was a perceived connection between "socialisation problems"—i.e. the chronic undersocialisation of children from disadvantaged families—and the functioning of the economic system. Strengthening the family was seen as the solution.

Other countries have adopted a less interventionist stance. In the Netherlands, where there appears to be little explicit concept of family policy, one writer described the situation as fragmented, relying on ad hoc solutions, and concluded that family policy cannot be co-ordinated when it does not exist. In the United Kingdom there has long been an assumed neutrality in relation to government intervention.

In Eastern European countries family policies cannot be fully understood without duly taking into account the fact that the main guarantees for the family are included in the Constitution itself. Thus, for example, the Constitution of Poland states, inter alia, that "the People's Republic of Poland, concerned for the development of the nation, protects the family, motherhood and the education of the young generation" and that "large families are under the special protection of the State".

Below we consider the four broad objectives of family policy in more detail.

The *demographic objective* of family policy is probably the most prevalent. As discussed in detail in Chapter 1, fertility levels in much of Europe are below replacement levels. In many countries widespread concern about increasing childlessness and fears of population decline — amounting sometimes to a demographic panic—have stemmed from anxiety over the consequences of changes in the age composition of the population, combined with the effects on national power and prestige. This concern with population has played an important role in stimulating an interest in family policies, although it has not always resulted in concrete action.

France is a particularly interesting example of a country where family policy in the past had very strong population objectives, but where there has been a reversal of motivations. The initial introduction in 1932 of cash family benefits was clearly a response to the "demographic crisis", as it was perceived. A second phase, starting around 1950, was characterised less by demographic concerns—France, like much of Europe, experienced a sudden "baby boom"—and more by specific social objectives such as helping poor and particularly vulnerable families. Starting in 1981, the third phase was again motivated by demographic concern; however, the policies designed in response were very different from the previous ones. The French Government officially abandoned the priority previously given to the third child; it sharply increased family allowances for two-child families. In turn, the new Government in 1986 reoriented cash family benefits so that they were less dependent on income, while again putting more emphasis on benefits directed towards large families.

The target groups of family policies in France have thus been radically altered several times in a span of 50 years. One might expect such frequent changes to provoke a certain feeling of uncertainty which could in turn deter some families from raising more children.

Partly because none of the countries in Europe—or anywhere in the world—have demonstrated convincingly that there are damaging long-term consequences of population stability or even of a small decline, and partly because of lack of evidence that family policy has had a significant impact on demographic changes, population objectives recently appear to have taken a lower priority in discussions of family policy in many countries. In a few countries, however, such as France and the Federal Republic of Germany, population goals have again assumed pride of place.

It should be added that some Eastern European countries, in particular the USSR, distinguish two kinds of social security measure in favour of families: first, means-tested benefits aimed at ensuring a decent standard of living for low-income families; and, second, non-means-tested benefits, such as special provisions for pregnant women and mothers, explicitly designed to achieve demographic goals.

The second goal, *the protection of children from poverty*, and the redistribution of income towards those with family responsibilities, has long been an objective of family policy in general, and social security policy in particular. Priorities in terms of smaller or larger families, one- or two-parent families, or more general "horizontal redistribution" (redistribution of income within economically active population groups) have varied between place and time, responding, at least partly, to demographic developments. The mechanisms adopted to pursue this objective have evolved likewise. Ireland and the USSR are two such examples. In Ireland legislation passed in 1984 and 1986 clearly put the emphasis on benefits for the largest and poorest families, with increased rates for the fifth and subsequent children. In the USSR a 1981 reform introduced a strong differential in the birth grant according to the child's position in the family. Thus, the amounts paid for the second and third children are now higher than those granted for the fourth and the fifth.

The objectives of *neutrality and freedom of choice* constitute the third main focus of European family policies. These are ambitious and idealistic aims, often in conflict with many of the past goals of family policy, as well as with some other aspects of social security.

This development is related to wider changes, in particular to the shift towards considering individuals, rather than family groups, as the basic unit for the purposes of social policy and social security. This shift, which has occurred mainly in the Scandinavian countries, has brought with it a recognition that individuals may make different choices, and that as a result greater diversity in family types and situations may develop. Implicitly, if not always explicitly, the role of the State has become to reduce the differences in the standard of living of families, and particularly of children. This may involve evening out circumstances between families with only one child and those with several children, between families with one or two parents, and between mothers who are in paid employment and those who are not.

A number of policy measures have been developed within this overall framework of "equalising the situation of all children", "supporting all types of family units", or simply of helping the most vulnerable families or those most in need. Many of these have been in the broadly defined area of maternity, and more recently paternity, provision. Again, they cannot but influence demographic development.

The fourth principal objective of family policy relates to *sex roles and the perceived interests of the labour market*. The aim may be to draw women into employment or, conversely, to provide incentives for them to leave it.

The goal of drawing women into the labour market is most commonly stated in Eastern European countries. Indeed, the Constitutions of many of these countries guarantee the employment of women and make the organisation of family policies to facilitate it a priority. In socialist countries state policies are usually based on constitutional guarantees for the employment of women, with priority for working mothers, and on a general employment policy, intended to prevent unemployment. This may have a direct influence on the way that families function in that it removes the tensions arising from a permanent threat of unemployment and the resulting loss of material resources for the maintenance of the family. These policies have led to very high women's labour force participation rates, which are estimated at around 45 per cent in all the Eastern European countries, with the exception of the USSR (51 per cent) and Yugoslavia (38 per cent). Special legislative provisions aim at improving the quality of life of women and families in terms of working hours, special leave and social services, to which reference will be made later in this chapter. Family policies are, therefore, both closely interwoven with, and explicitly used to promote, labour market objectives.

In Western Europe the goal is less explicitly stated, but for many countries it is an important objective. In the Federal Republic of Germany, for example, there is increased recognition that the constraints imposed by family responsibilities on professionally educated women have public costs as well as private ones. If, for example, only one-third of all female specialists actually work in their profession—as is the case for physicians in the Federal Republic of Germany—then one may argue that the investment in training represented by the other two-thirds has been wasted.

Financial incentives to encourage the return to the one-earner family have nevertheless seemed at various times an advantageous proposition in many countries. Some have seen this as an attempt to reduce the extent of male unemployment, while others have seen it as desirable in terms of the upbringing of children. Although this objective is a subject of recurrent discussion, no country has been explicit about its intentions to reduce women's role in the labour market.

The nature and goals of family policy are, then, many and various. Some of the developments in family policy will be discussed later on. But next we turn to the demographic developments that shape the context of family policy, while perhaps in turn being shaped by that policy.

DEMOGRAPHIC DEVELOPMENTS OF SPECIAL IMPORTANCE FOR FAMILY POLICY

Major demographic changes that directly influence the relationship between family policy, social security and demography have taken place over the past two decades. These include five principal areas of change:
— falling birth rates and smaller families;
— fewer marriages, more cohabitation and more illegitimate births;
— an increase in divorce, remarriage and reconstituted families;
— an increase in the proportions of one-parent families;
— an ageing population.
We examine each of these areas below.

The *changes in total fertility rates* for a number of European countries between 1965 and 1986 were shown in table 1. Each country has experienced a fall in births—and often a dramatic one: the change in the crude birth rate has varied between 10 and 46 per cent. The decline has been greater in Western European countries than in Eastern European ones, and the crude birth rate was on average lower in 1986 in the former than in the latter; 20 years ago the reverse was the case. In two-thirds of the countries listed in table 1, total fertility rates are below replacement level.

The decline·in fertility is due to a number of factors, as discussed in Chapter 1. It has resulted partly from many countries having smaller generations reaching the fertile age groups, and partly from social and economic policies.

In countries which have sought to encourage births, one result has been for a proportion of births to occur sooner: couples responded by having their children earlier and at shorter intervals. These children were then "missing" from the subsequent birth rate statistics. The average number of children planned has also been declining over the past two decades, and the rate of one-child families has increased dramatically.

The second important demographic change is a *decline in the marriage rate* and, at least in some Western countries, a higher age at marriage. While it is difficult to find data in a form that allows precise comparisons to be made across Europe,[2] the trend towards fewer marriages is clear in both Eastern and Western countries, although at a slower pace in the former.

The other side of the coin is, of course, the *rise in the incidence of cohabitation*, which is much more widespread and seems more generally accepted by public opinion. For some couples, particularly for young ones, it may be a temporary arrangement which will eventually lead to marriage. For others, it seems to be an alternative to the institution of marriage. A related issue is the birth rate within the non-married population, i.e. the illegitimacy rate. Table 5 shows that this rose— sometimes dramatically—in 20 out of 25 European countries between 1972 and 1980.

The third group of demographic changes concerns the *rise in the incidence of divorce*. Again it is difficult to distinguish between cause and effect: divorce laws have been liberalised in most European countries, partly in response to the rise in the breakdown of marriages; on the other hand, the new liberalised laws may well have led to a further rise. One in three European marriages is now likely to end in divorce. Remarriage rates, however, are rising and many families are thus reconstituted in the traditional mould.

The fourth set of changes follows from the previous ones: the decline in marriage and the increase in divorce have resulted—where there is no remarriage or cohabitation—in an *increase in one-parent families*. Table 6 shows the number and proportion of single parents in certain European countries. Although the table is based on family allowance schemes rather than on the entire population, the increase is clear and consistent in every country.

The last important demographic change concerns the *ageing population*, again to be found in both Western and Eastern European countries. This affects family policies in a number of ways. First, it means that an increased proportion of social security resources and expenditure will have to be allocated to ensuring an adequate income for the elderly, thereby competing with the amount available for family support. Second, it raises the whole question of family support for the elderly: What is the role of the family today in caring for elderly people? At a time when some countries may be seeking to withdraw resources from the support

Table 5. Illegitimate live births in selected European countries, 1972 and 1980 (in percentages)

Country	1972	1980
Austria	13.7	17.8
Belgium	3.0	3.4
Bulgaria	9.9	10.9
Czechoslovakia	5.2	4.9
Denmark	14.4	33.2
Finland	6.7	13.1
France	7.8	11.4
German Democratic Republic	16.2	22.8
Germany, Federal Republic of	6.0	7.6
Greece	1.2	1.4
Iceland	32.3	39.7
Ireland	2.9	3.6
Italy	2.5	3.9
Luxembourg	4.2	6.0
Malta	1.3	1.0
Netherlands	1.9	3.4
Norway	8.7	14.5
Poland	4.9	4.7
Portugal	7.2	7.2[1]
San Marino	1.0	3.5[2]
Spain	1.4	2.2[3]
Sweden	25.1	39.7
Switzerland	3.7	4.4
United Kingdom	8.4	10.7
Yugoslavia	8.1	8.0[2]

[1] 1975 figures. [2] 1978 figures. [3] 1976 figures.

Source: United Nations: *Demographic Yearbook, 1981* (New York, 1983), table 32.

of families, these same countries may simultaneously be expecting the families to increase their support for the elderly generation. This aspect is dealt with more fully elsewhere in the book.

Thus each of the five demographic trends has presented major challenges to the families of the 1980s. The combined effects of the changes may be considered in relation to two countries—Sweden and

Table 6. Number and proportion of single parents[1] in selected European countries, 1970s and 1980s

Country	Year	No.	%	Year	No.	%
Austria	1971	123 221	13.1	1983	152 900	15.9
Belgium	1970	214 707	14.7	1981	245 291	16.8
Czechoslovakia	1976	103 767	3.7	1980	147 949	6.1
Denmark	1973	71 840	9.3	1983	85 899	15.7
France	1975	776 000	6.3	1982	887 000[2]	6.7
Germany, Fed. Rep. of	—	—	—	1980	341 000	21.0
Hungary	1973	286 200	17.0	1980	341 000	21.0
Poland	1970	1 042 900	19.1	1978	1 249 500	20.8
Switzerland	1970	81 520	10.4	1980	108 561	12.8
United Kingdom	1971	570 000	8.0	1981	925 500	12.0

[1] Total number receiving benefits from family allowance schemes during the past decade and their proportion as a percentage of the total number of two-parent families. [2] The total number of single parents, including those who were not entitled to children's benefits, was 1,658,000.

Source: International Social Security Association (ISSA): *Family benefits provided for one-parent families*, Report submitted to the 22nd General Assembly, Montreal, September 1986 (mimeographed), p. 4.

Romania—and these are summarised in table 7. In Sweden the divorce rate has risen, and large families with more than three children are now rare. How far the Swedish pattern represents the future prospect for other European countries must be a matter of speculation, but most of the European countries are moving in that direction. The case of Romania shows, however, that such a trend might in certain cases be resisted; divorce, against which this country introduced quite restrictive measures in 1972, is without any doubt the most striking example.

To some observers, these changes have been interpreted as "bad news", the increased instability of the family leading almost automatically to a decrease in the average birth rate. Questions about the possible decline of the family have been asked: "Is it an endangered species threatened with extinction?" was the widespread concern in the early 1980s.[3] Furthermore, is it possible that government policies may themselves be contributing to this instability? Is there any evidence that measures designed to support families are in fact breaking them up?

To others, the same changes in family structures have been seen in a different light, as part of a continuing pattern of change. There is much evidence of diversity in families of the past. Historians, for example, have

Table 7. Some demographic changes in Sweden and Romania

Marriages

Year	Marriages contracted per 1,000 inhabitants	
	Sweden	Romania
1941–50	9.0	10.4
1971–75	5.0	8.1
1980	4.5	8.2
1985	n.a.	7.1

Divorces

Year	Sweden (per 100,000 married women)	Romania (per 100,000 inhabitants)
1958	493	196
1970	1 449	39
1979	11 135	163
1985	n.a.	143

Families with children by number of children (percentages)

No. of children	Sweden (1979)	Romania (families with birth during the year 1985)
1	44.0	37.9
2	41.7	32.0
3	11.6	14.7
4+	12.4	15.3

n.a. = not available.

Sources: T. Eriksen: "Health protection systems and contemporary family needs in Sweden", in ISSA: *Social security and family policy*, European Series No. 8 (Geneva, 1983), tables 2, 4 and 5; *Anuarul Statistic al Republicii Socialiste Românica* (Bucharest, 1986).

demonstrated that there were large numbers of one-parent families in previous centuries; widowhood was common, as was male migration, seasonal travel in search of work and the abandonment of wife and children.[4] It is only the legalised form of divorce that is new.

Migration—and especially internal migration—may also be seen as having an unfavourable effect on fertility rates. There may be two major reasons for this: first, internal migration chiefly concerns male workers, thus destroying the traditional family pattern in the places of origin; second, migrant workers and their families coming from less-developed areas (where the average number of children is as a rule higher) tend to adopt quite rapidly the reproductive patterns corresponding to their new place of residence, thus contributing to the overall fall in the birth rate. In turn, urban patterns may influence the rural population, especially in countries where urban and rural areas overlap. This may be seen in the Yugoslav context, for example, where rural dwellers who work in towns have tended to adopt the urban reproductive patterns, or in the German Democratic Republic, where demographers state that in the mid-1970s deep changes in the reproductive behaviour of the rural population took place, bringing birth rates close to the much lower level of the urban population.[5]

The emerging consensus among demographers is nevertheless that fears about increasing instability are not well founded. Some specialists have stated that the family is by no means in decay. What may be happening is that new types of families have come into prominence and that there are significant changes in the structure and composition of families, and in family functions and roles.

What then is the family today? The nuclear family is still the core. However, the parents may not have a marriage certificate; or they may have two or more certificates: marriage, divorce, remarriage. At times the family may consist only of mother and child; however, single parenthood tends in most cases to be a temporary phase rather than a permanent state. One-child families are more common than in the past, and large families are declining fast. Families with children from previous, as well as present, partnerships are becoming more common. At the same time, it is worth noting that class and income differences, which may not affect the external characteristics of families, still have a fundamental influence on the standard of living of the family. While demographic developments have meant that the European family may well be characterised by increasing change and diversity, there is little evidence that it is characterised by crisis.

DEVELOPMENTS IN FAMILY POLICY

Family policies are characterised by change. Changes in objectives, priorities and orientation are all important; equally, changes have occurred in types and methods of provision. Family policies are responses to many social, economic and demographic developments; they also help to shape these developments. In short, they are multidimensional and multipurpose. In this section we first look at the context of recent changes and then analyse the variety of changes that have occurred.

In addition to the demographic developments considered earlier, other important influences set the context for the development of family policies. First, there is the general economic situation. Economic difficulties must be the starting-point for a discussion of all policy developments in the 1980s. As a recent ILO publication argued,[6] the sudden concentration of attention on social security, and in particular on the legitimacy of state protection, is a reaction to economic difficulties, increasing unemployment and declining industries—which have at times been referred to as "the world-wide economic crisis". The dual way in which social security both affects and is affected by developments within society is reflected clearly in the economic crisis. Increasingly heavy demands are being made on the social security system precisely at a time when contributions are declining.

Economic difficulties affect family policies in two general ways. First, there is a tendency to cut back on public expenditure; this may, although it does not always, include family policies. In Western European countries "austerity measures" have not been uncommon. Belgium, for example, introduced "adjustments" to family allowances in 1984 which meant that age supplements were deferred or withdrawn and the normal indexation of benefits for the first two children was abolished. In Denmark economic difficulties were one of the major reasons for the introduction of a means test for family allowances in 1976, and for changes in the price index regulations in 1982. (It must be added that the means test was abolished in 1984.) In most countries in Eastern Europe, however, the development of family policy has not been dependent on economic growth. Poland is one example where there was a significant increase in expenditure on social benefits in the early 1980s, specifically to protect those families and individuals who were experiencing the greatest degree of economic difficulty. Furthermore, over the years most Eastern European countries have maintained a great stability in the proportion of social expenditure devoted to family benefits—or even an increase of that share—although the amount of pensions paid varies in pace with the ageing of the population. This stability may be seen as political determination at least to maintain—and if possible to improve—state subsidies to families, in order, inter alia, to counteract the general trend towards lower fertility rates.

Two conclusions can be drawn on the economic context: first, the economic situation has important implications for family policy, and, second, countries may respond either by increasing their expenditure or by reducing it.

The second general development that has had an effect on family policies is the increase in the number of women in the labour force and the related concern with the equal treatment of men and women. This rise in women's labour force participation has been widespread throughout Europe, and in spite of the economic recession and high levels of unemployment among women, the numbers continue to grow. In the countries of Eastern Europe, the large majority of women have been and continue to be employed.

The increased employment of women has raised a number of problems which have required responses in terms of family policy. These have included arrangements covering maternity leave and rights of mothers to guaranteed reinstatement, as well as those relating the calculation of pension entitlement to the responsibilities of child bearing. It is important to note that higher labour force participation, rather than theories of equality between men and women, was the original impetus for many of the family policies which have been developed in European countries.

However, the question of equality was raised when the treatment of married women as dependants in the social security system became too visibly incongruous with the actual labour market situation; the same incongruity became apparent in the tax system. As a result, a number of national and international instruments, adopted in recent years, have created the framework for legislative reform and the development of family policies.

The present situation is a changing one. On the one hand, the concept of female dependency, which dominated the early development of many social security systems, remains entrenched in many ways. Many policies still offer the family protection through the insurance of the (male) bread-winner. On the other hand, there has been increased recognition of different kinds of family, with different kinds of needs. Recent developments in family policy have been much concerned with reorienting the old model towards new and more relevant models of family needs.

A third important influence on the development of family policies has inevitably been the national philosophy and history of each country. Family policies have often been developed in response to specific national perceptions of problems, priorities and issues, and these must be recognised in order to understand the developments that have occurred. As a report of the International Social Security Association argued in 1986: "The extension to both parents of leave related to maternity or child care has proceeded at a pace that has varied from country to country: this is an instructive example of the connection between social security and social custom."[7]

The Scandinavian countries, which are often regarded as promoting—and responding to—change in this field, have generally led the attempt to recognise greater equality between parents with regard to family responsibilities. They have also been very active in the trend towards treating unmarried couples in the same way as married ones, for the purpose of family benefits, as well as reformulating the social security rights of divorced people. These developments are all part of a national philosophy—which perhaps can be characterised as supporting a wide range of models, personal choices and types of family structure. In contrast, other countries' national values involve a more directive approach.

The concept of parental leave has, nevertheless, now reached countries where the social status of women was in the past regarded as less favourable than in the Nordic countries, for example. Thus, Portugal and Greece in 1984 introduced provisions aiming at granting leave to either parent in case of birth (Portugal) or in case of illness of the child (both countries).

The right to parental leave is also recognised in some socialist countries, such as the Soviet Union, where leave in order to care for a sick child may be taken by either the mother or the father—although in fact, in most cases, it is still actually taken by the mother.

TYPES OF FAMILY BENEFITS AND METHODS OF PROVISION

Cash family benefits

Cash family benefits in Europe (otherwise known as family allowances) are many and various. They are administered by ministries of social welfare, social insurance, labour and finance, by family allowance funds and by trade union councils. They may be universal or employment related, flat-rate or means-tested, available to all children or only to those in larger or one-parent families; the allowance may be the same for each child or related to the child's age or position in the family. The value of the family allowance varies greatly, as shown in table 8, ranging from 3 per cent of average earnings to 25 per cent; Hungary, Bulgaria and Czechoslovakia had the highest relative levels in 1980. The changes in

Table 8. Family allowances for two children as a percentage of average remuneration, selected countries, 1980

Country	%
Austria	16.9
Belgium	10.7
Bulgaria	22.2
Czechoslovakia	20.0
Denmark	3.0[1]
France	6.5
German Democratic Republic	3.9
Germany, Federal Republic of	6.6[1]
Hungary	24.9
Italy	5.4
Netherlands	9.0
Norway	6.4[1]
Poland	19.6[2]
Romania	17.0
Sweden	8.7[1]
Switzerland	6.9
United Kingdom	8.2

[1] Figures for 1981. [2] Figures for 1984.

Sources: ILO: *Year Book of Labour Statistics, 1981* (Geneva); Poland, Institute of Labour and Social Affairs: *Comparative data in the field of social policy, 1982* (Warsaw).

levels will be considered in more detail below, but first we describe the changes that have occurred in the form of family allowances.

Recent changes

Several countries made substantial changes in their family allowance systems in the late 1970s or the 1980s. In *France* three new benefits were introduced in 1985: a "young child allowance" for children under the age of 3, which is universal for nine months and then means-tested; a universal "single-parent allowance" (which had previously been wholly means-tested); and a "parental education allowance", paid for up to two years (three years as from 1987) to a previously employed parent who stops employment to raise a third or subsequent child. The rates of allowance for second and subsequent children were also substantially increased. These measures came in addition to those adopted in 1978 and 1980, aiming at granting to families with three or more children a kind of means-tested guaranteed family income. In the *Federal Republic of Germany* there was a shift away from universal benefits for larger families, with the levels being cut for third and subsequent children; but increases were introduced for low-income families. These provisions were introduced in two stages, in 1981 and 1982, as part of general measures designed to promote budget savings. *Ireland* introduced a new, supplementary, income-tested benefit for poorer families, to which reference was made earlier in this chapter. *Italy* developed a supplement for those on low incomes but also reduced benefits for those on high incomes. *Spain* implemented in 1985 a reform which reorganised the existing system and redistributed resources among the various fields of social protection related to the needs of the families. *Sweden* maintained its universal system but provided higher increases for larger families. As already mentioned, *Denmark* first introduced, but then abolished, a means test for family allowances.

Thus, in these Western European countries, changes took place which in different ways were designed mainly to focus family allowances more on those in greatest need. The objective may be interpreted as primarily concerned with the alleviation of poverty through income distribution; only in France do the developments embody any discernible demographic objective.

In Eastern European countries, and as far as cash family benefits are concerned, the main trend during recent years was towards consolidating and improving existing provisions—with the exception of those especially designed for women at work, some of which will be listed below, under the heading "Parental support".

The most salient features are the following. In *Poland*, since 1980, an increased interest has been shown in cash benefits for children, which in 1985 represented 55.7 per cent of social benefits, as against 47.6 per cent in 1980. In *Bulgaria* the increase in family allowances decided on in 1985 was limited to the second and third children in the family, whereas in *Czechoslovakia*, also in 1985, family allowances were increased by the same amount irrespective of the child's position in the family, although the initial amounts of benefits were higher according to this position. In *Romania* the "mothers' benefit", which initially was granted to mothers having reared five or more children, was extended in 1986 to mothers with three or more children; it amounted monthly to roughly 13 per cent of the average wage for three and four children, and to 16 per cent for five or more children. In the *USSR* it was decided in January 1987 to exempt young couples during their first year of marriage from the payment of special taxes for people without children (usually amounting to 6–10 per cent of salary). This kind of tax, which is not uncommon in Eastern European countries, may be seen as a strong incentive to marriage and fecundity, especially where general taxes on revenue are very low or even non-existent.

The issue of selectivity

A related development in family policies has been the debate over the advantages and disadvantages of selectivity (i.e. focusing family policies on some families only, selected on the basis of income or composition) in contrast to a more universally based policy. Selectivity is often a response to financial pressures and is frequently thought to be a cost-effective way of reducing expenditure. However, selectivity is not "cost free", as is sometimes assumed, as financial savings may have a social cost.

Selectivity may operate in different ways. Some forms of selectivity have explicitly demographic objectives, as when it is decided to give differential support to large or small families; but selectivity related to family size, which tended to characterise population policy in the past, is becoming less widespread. Selectivity now tends to be on the basis of identifying those families most in need, usually by means of some combination of demographic and income-related factors. In one review of Eastern European family policies, it was argued that—

bearing in mind the opportunities offered by social policies and the limitations imposed on them by economic considerations, East European countries will no doubt pay even closer attention in future to directing social benefits towards the families in greatest need, i.e. large families, single-parent families, young couples and families with low incomes.[8]

The general trend in the development of family policy in Eastern European countries in the near future could therefore be towards a high degree of selectivity, as shown by the measures already taken in the USSR and in Romania, for example. It must be stressed, however, that should there be greater selectivity in Eastern European countries in the next few years, this would be on top of a well-developed general support for the family.

By contrast, in Western European countries, where the debate on selectivity has been the most vocal, a comprehensive, well-developed family policy system is often lacking, and the planned selectivity may have high social costs. It is interesting to note that a means test on family allowances was introduced in Yugoslavia as early as 1968, with the goal of improving benefits in kind and services for families by reducing expenditure on cash benefits.

Changes in the value of cash family benefits

Next we turn to changes in the value of, and expenditure on, cash family benefits (family allowances). Table 9 shows clearly that their value, in terms of purchasing power, varied widely among OECD countries between 1960 and 1984, as did their annual growth rate. In 1984 the actual value, at purchasing power parities, ranged from US$77 in Greece to US$1,305 in France. The highest absolute levels of support occurred in France, Austria and Denmark. In real terms all increased between the years 1960 and 1984. France and Sweden, both of which had relatively high values in 1960, increased proportionately at a slower rate than countries such as Norway or the Netherlands, which had a low

Table 9. Value of family allowances at purchasing power parities[1], selected OECD countries, 1960–84 (US$ at 1980 prices per person aged under 15)

Country	1960	1973	1979	1984	Annual average growth rate (%)	
					1960–84	1979–84
Austria	295	522	1 092	1 012	5.3	− 1.5
Denmark	145	762	847	1 012	8.4	3.6
Finland	151	164	313	383	4.0	4.1
France	657	878	1 110	1 305	2.9	3.3
Germany, Fed. Rep. of	61	128	636	529	9.4	− 3.6
Greece	n.a.	41	86	77	n.a.	− 2.2
Ireland	106	206	152	217[2]	3.2	8.0
Italy	393	367	344	423	0.3	4.2
Netherlands	215	618	769	914	6.2	3.5
Norway	122	414	377	684	7.4	12.7
Portugal	n.a.	177	100	102	n.a.	0.2
Spain	n.a.	299	117	60	n.a.	− 12.5
Sweden	408	806	927	808	2.9	− 2.7
Switzerland	30	95	144	177	7.7	4.2
United Kingdom	137	230	643	855	7.9	5.8

n.a. = not available.

[1] Purchasing power parities are rates of exchange adjusted for differences in price levels in each country. If cash family benefits have the same value, this means that they represent the same amount of goods and services in the two countries.
[2] Figures for 1983.

Source: R. Varley: *The government household transfer data base, 1960–84*, Working Paper No. 36 (Paris, OECD, Department of Economics and Statistics, 1986), table 10.

starting-point but a high annual average growth rate. Table 8, as already mentioned, enables partial comparison between Western and Eastern European countries.

For the OECD countries listed in table 9, family allowances are shown in table 10 as a percentage of total social security and welfare benefits. In 11 of the 15 countries, family benefits represented a lower proportion of total social security and welfare expenditure in 1984 than in 1960. When one compares 1984 with 1979, family allowances amounted to a lower proportion in 14 of the countries. However, the total expenditure on social security had also increased over that period, principally because of higher unemployment. Although the proportionally lower expenditure on family allowances indicates a relative decline in their importance in social security as a whole, it should be remembered that in most cases this represents a declining proportion of an increasing budget. This, however, does not apply to the same extent to

Table 10. Family allowances as a percentage of total social security and welfare benefits, selected OECD countries, 1960–84

Country	1960	1973	1979	1984
Austria	12.8	11.5	14.7	11.1
Denmark	11.7	17.8	12.8	11.8
Finland	25.0	7.5	9.2	8.3
France	32.9	18.9	14.7	13.9
Germany, Fed. Rep. of	2.1	2.5	7.3	4.9
Greece	3.6[1]	4.1	5.4	3.4[2]
Ireland	20.9	15.8	9.2	8.7[2]
Italy	29.0	10.3	6.7	5.3
Netherlands	15.9	12.1	8.7	8.4
Norway	14.6	12.4	7.4	10.2
Portugal	35.3[1]	30.1	8.8	6.6
Spain	n.a.	22.1	4.6	1.8
Sweden	18.0	13.1	9.1	7.0
Switzerland	3.2	2.6	2.9	2.8
United Kingdom	11.3	10.3	18.3	16.6

n.a. = not available.
[1] Figures for 1962. [2] Figures for 1983.
Source: Varley, op. cit., and author's own calculations.

Eastern European countries, where it appears to be a general political decision at least to maintain the relative share of family benefits within the overall social budget. Thus, in Romania, the share of benefits for children amounted in 1985 to 15.5 per cent of the state social and cultural budget, against 13.0 per cent in 1965; the corresponding percentages were 24.6 and 27.5 in Bulgaria, and 28 and 23 in Czechoslovakia.

The factors underlying changes in expenditure on family allowances have also been analysed for the OECD countries; the results are presented in table 11. The analysis seeks to explain the changes as a proportion of gross domestic product (GDP) in terms of changes in:

(a) the proportion of the total population who are children (aged under 16);

(b) the ratio of the number of family allowance beneficiaries to children under 16 ("coverage");

(c) the ratio of family allowances per beneficiary to GDP per head (the "transfer ratio").

Table 11. Explanation of changes in family allowances, selected OECD countries, 1960–80 (in percentages)

Country	Change in proportion of population aged under 16		Change in ratio of beneficiaries to children under 16		Change in transfer ratio[1]		Change in total expenditure on family allowances	
	1960–70	1970–80	1960–70	1970–80	1960–70	1970–80	1960–70	1970–80
Belgium	−	−15	+10	+12	+36	−	+50	−5
Finland	−19	−16	+1	−9	−32	+41	−45	+17
France	−6	−10	+8	+3	−24	−8	−22	−15
Germany, Fed. Rep. of	+9	−24	+113	+216	−37	−6	+45	+115
Italy	−	−11	−18	+29	−4	−48	−20	−41
Netherlands	−9	−16	+67	+17	−4	−6	+46	−7
Norway	−6	−9	+106	+1	−65	−22	−31	−29
Sweden	−7	−4	+44	+65	−30	−24	−5	+19
United Kingdom	+3	−12	+12	+113	+17	+7	+35	+101

[1] Change in ratio of family allowances per beneficiary to GDP per head.

Source: Adapted from P. Saunders and F. Klau: "The role of the public sector", Special issue of *OECD Economic Studies* (Paris), No. 4, Spring 1985, table 37.

Thus, for example, in Belgium between 1960 and 1970 the proportion of children in the population remained the same but beneficiaries rose relative to the number of children by 10 per cent and the average family allowance increased by 36 per cent more than GDP per head; the result was an increase of 50 per cent in total expenditure on family allowances relative to GDP.

Between 1960 and 1970, in the nine countries studied, family allowance expenditure relative to GDP increased in four and declined in five. The proportion of children in the population did not change greatly, except in Finland, but in four countries—the Federal Republic of Germany, the Netherlands, Norway and Sweden—the coverage of family allowances greatly increased. Most significantly, perhaps, in seven countries the level of family allowances rose more slowly than GDP per head.

Between 1970 and 1980 the pattern was somewhat different. The number of children fell relative to the total population in all nine countries. The Federal Republic of Germany, Sweden and the United Kingdom substantially increased their coverage of family allowances: in the United Kingdom, for example, this was because family allowances for second and subsequent children were replaced by child benefit for all children. The transfer ratio fell in six countries and rose only in Finland and the United Kingdom.

One problem with comparing the levels of family allowances alone is that this fails to take account of the tax treatment of families. In some countries family allowances are taxed, and in others not; in some countries there are tax allowances for children, and in others not. The effect of taking tax into account is illustrated in table 12 for selected EEC countries.[9] Comparing gross and net income support changes the picture somewhat—Luxembourg, for example, moved from fifth to second position. Belgium, France and the Netherlands, however, remain the countries that provided the most income support.

The relationship between taxation and family allowances should not of course be seen as a major factor as far as demographic trends are concerned. Nor, however, should the actual impact of this factor be underestimated in areas such as the distinction made within the tax system between couples who are married and those living on a consensual basis. It has been argued in some Western European countries that the lack of neutrality of certain tax systems favouring non-married couples over married ones could be seen as one of the factors leading to a decrease in marriages and, indirectly, to a corresponding decline in births. On the other hand, mention has already been made of the special taxes affecting families with no children in some countries, which may have positive effects on fertility rates of the populations concerned.

Table 12. Gross and net income support for two-child families, selected EEC countries, 1980[1]

Country	Family allowance as % of gross average earnings	Additional income[2] as % of net income of couple with no children on average earnings
Belgium	14.1 (1)	21.7 (1)
Denmark	3.9 (7)	5.8 (8)
France	8.4 (4)	13.3 (3)
Germany, Fed. Rep. of	6.0 (6)	8.8 (6)
Ireland	2.2 (9)	6.5 (7)
Italy	3.1 (8)	4.2 (9)
Luxembourg	7.0 (5)	16.5 (2)
Netherlands	9.1 (2)	13.1 (4)
United Kingdom	8.7 (3)	11.5 (5)

[1] Figures in parentheses show rank order. [2] After family allowances, social security contributions and income tax of a couple with two children compared with a couple with no children.

Source: J. Bradshaw and D. Piachaud: *Child support in the European Community* (London, Bedford Square Press, 1980), tables 13.5 and 18.2.

Child-care services

Although a comparison of countries according to levels of family allowances may be interesting, it does not present the whole picture. In fact, services are an integral part of family policies in many countries. The USSR, for example, has an extensive network of family support services, which it has developed over the years. There are 128,000 kindergartens and crèches, providing for more than 14 million children; parents can choose between day care, 24-hour care and sanatorium care (two- to three-months' stay in preventive semi-medical premises with school facilities, where mothers may in some cases accompany the child). Approximately 60 per cent of schools provide after-school facilities for 11 million children, where teachers supervise children until their parents return from work. Sixteen million children spend their holidays in state-subsidised camps. It may be noted that up to 1984 only 20 per cent of the vouchers for holidays in pioneer camps were fully free of charge; this percentage is now 50 per cent, while the amount charged for the other 50 per cent of vouchers corresponds to only 20 per cent of the actual cost.

The provision of such services and facilities is fairly widespread in the

Table 13. Social benefits in cash and in kind in selected Eastern European countries, 1980 (in percentages)

Country	Cash	Kind	Total
Bulgaria	51.1	48.9	100.0
Czechoslovakia	50.4	49.6	100.0
German Democratic Republic[1]	37.2	62.8	100.0
Hungary	59.0	41.0	100.0
Poland	47.6	52.4	100.0
USSR	39.5	60.5	100.0

[1] 1981 figures.

Source: Ewa Borowczyk: "State social policy in favour of the family in East European countries", in *International Social Security Review* (Geneva, ISSA), 2/1986, table 3.

countries of Eastern Europe. As shown in table 13, among expenditure on social benefits amounting to between 20 and 30 per cent of national income, benefits in kind, which include facilities for children, accounted for between 40 and 60 per cent of the total in 1980 and 1981. This represents a far higher proportion than in most Western European countries (with the notable exception of Denmark), although the figures may not be directly comparable (see table 14).

The emphasis on child-care services in Eastern Europe is the consequence of two important ways of looking at the family. First, family contingencies are seen not in terms of separate groups of families, but as stages in the individual life cycle. This approach largely avoids the whole problem of stigmatising certain families and labelling them as "deprived". It is not only "incomplete" or "disadvantaged" families who need these services, but all families. Second, families are viewed far more as being part of public life: this is contrast to some Western countries, where the family is still identified with private life and individualism. As a result, the communal education of children became quite early on a part of social and family policy, which adopted a pragmatic approach to the support of families, with considerable national investment in facilities and services.

A special mention should be made of the housing problem, which remains one of the major concerns of families, and particularly of large families, in any European country. Most of the Eastern European countries have brought into force general regulations enabling large families or young married couples to benefit from high priority in housing allocation or from state loans for housing purposes. Although

Table 14. Social benefits in cash and in kind in selected Western European countries, 1980 (in percentages)[1]

Country	Cash	Kind	Total
Belgium	73.8	26.2	100.0
Denmark	54.1	45.9	100.0
France	69.6	30.6	100.0
Germany, Federal Republic of	71.8	28.2	100.0
Ireland	61.3	38.7	100.0
Italy	67.5	32.5	100.0
Luxembourg	79.0	21.0	100.0
Netherlands	77.4	22.6	100.0
United Kingdom	68.2	31.8	100.0
Europe (nine countries)	70.5	29.5	100.0

[1] These rates are not directly comparable with those in table 13, owing to differences in concepts such as "social benefits" and "social budget".

Source: Estimates of the Second European Social Budget (1976–80), Commission of the European Communities.

these special provisions may be seen as slightly marginal to the traditional concept of family policies in the field of social security, they provide an example of how the State may at least help individuals to realise their aspirations regarding the average desired number of children. In the German Democratic Republic, for example, 73,359 credits were granted in 1985 to young married couples (representing a total of 483 million marks) as against 29,594 credits in 1972 (146 million marks).

In addition to the debates on the principles underlying family policy, much discussion has taken place in the past decade on the concept of parental support, which is considered next.

Parental support

There are over 90 million employed women in Europe—including 40 million in the USSR. One of the earliest forms of family policy was to provide them with a prescribed period of maternity leave, ensuring security of employment before and after the birth of a child. Such maternity protection continues to play an important part in family policies throughout Europe. This is evident from the introduction of new measures, the improvement of existing standards, the extension of coverage to new groups, increases in the length of leave, higher rates of benefit and so on. The underlying motivation, however, might be seen less as the active promotion of child bearing and more as an attempt to stop employment conditions from deterring those families who want a child from having one. The aim is thus one of keeping options open, while bearing in mind the demographic objectives commonly pursued by many European governments.

Extended leave after the birth of a child was pioneered in Hungary some 20 years ago, and then became common both in Eastern and Western European countries. The leave may be paid or unpaid, and its length varies from six months to three years; this length may be different according to the child's position in the family, as in the case of the German Democratic Republic, where it is extended from one year for the first two children to 18 months for the third child. Mention should also be made of paid leave granted to mothers or fathers for looking after a sick child. In this field, too, the socialist countries may be seen as pioneers, followed by some Western European countries in recent years, where statutory provisions have often followed earlier ones included in enterprise or branch collective agreements. The right to paid leave may be limited either to a global number of days per year, as in Norway (ten days) or to a number of days per illness, as in the USSR (seven days, due to be increased to 14 days). The right to this kind of leave may be means-tested, as in Portugal. It is usually limited to children under 8 or 10 years of age, but may be extended until the child's 14th birthday, as in the German Democratic Republic.

Parental insurance and parental leave are the most recent developments in this area of family policy. This subject was dealt with by the ILO within the framework of the Workers with Family Responsibilities Convention (No. 156), and Recommendation (No. 165), both adopted in 1981. Sweden is particularly advanced in this respect, family policy being often regarded as part of a general effort to even out differences in living standards between different periods of the life cycle and to achieve a more or less equitable allocation of the cost of children among the whole of the active generation. Neutrality is an important objective in Sweden, as a result of which maternity insurance has been superseded by parental insurance, which allows parents to choose for themselves which of them stays at home and cares for a child for the first six months, or whether they choose to share the time together.

Various other measures similarly act to enable both parents to continue in employment as well as being involved in the care of their children, if that is their wish. This type of family policy is very far from the original model of encouraging single-earner families with a large number of children.

Parental, in contrast to maternal, leave is gaining widespread acceptance as a policy measure which serves a number of useful objectives such as the well-being of the child, the involvement of the father in the family and the reduction in the number of people in the workforce. One variant of parental insurance is the entitlement of the parents of young children to a reduction in their normal working hours.

Caring for children may have consequences at the other end of the age spectrum. Pensions have hitherto tended to be based on income-related contributions, but some countries have begun to recognise the need to provide pension benefits that are independent of, or at least proportionally greater than, contributions. Measures to achieve this include pension supplements for women who have reared children, and the inclusion of the period of pregnancy as a contributory period, even though contributions are not actually made. The most recent discussions consider including further periods of child care ("the home responsibility years") as contributory.

Thus, in France, mothers (not fathers) are granted a supplementary two-year insurance period for each child reared for at least nine years before his or her 16th birthday; furthermore, any insured person (male or female) with at least three children is granted a 10 per cent pension supplement. In the German Democratic Republic women who have reared one or two children are granted a one-year insurance supplement per child; those having reared at least three children for eight years or more are granted a three-year supplement per child. In addition, since 1984, women who give birth to five or more children are granted a full minimum pension with only 15 years of insurance (instead of 45). Those are just examples of the various provisions for mothers appearing in different European pension schemes. Ways of combining welfare and insurance principles within pension schemes and other family-related policies are increasingly being sought, as is the case in many other branches of social security.

Family policy does not, of course, end with cash family benefits, child-care provisions and parental support policies—although these are probably the policy areas with most significance for social security. Other policy measures—such as those concerned with housing, equal opportunities and low pay—are of great importance to families; they affect, and are affected by, demographic developments. Yet to consider all these areas would be to stray from our central theme.

Having considered recent policy developments, this chapter now turns to their possible effects on demographic development.

THE EFFECTS OF FAMILY POLICIES

Developments in family policy have been largely a response to demographic, social and economic changes. But there is also concern about the effects of these developments. How far have they shaped, rather than having been shaped by, changes in society?

Social and economic policies rarely have straightforward effects on modern societies. Such policies interact with policies in other spheres, as well as with other developments within European post-industrial society. The result is a complex matrix of conditions and behaviour, most of which cannot be attributable to any specific influence.

This is particularly true of family policies. The variety of social and economic policies which affect family and household formation is great, and their objectives may conflict. At least one writer has concluded that most of the impact of government policy on demographic behaviour has been unintended.[10]

The results of a study conducted in Hungary on a longitudinal basis[11] provide an interesting illustration of this. On three occasions during the past decades the Hungarian authorities took strong population policy measures explicitly aimed at stemming the decline in fertility in the country. These measures were broadly as follows: in 1967 introduction of the child-care allowance enabling economically active women to care for their young children at home until the child reached the age of 3; in 1974 increase of maternal support to families with children, improvement of health care for pregnant women, organisation of training in family planning and extension of the basic network of children's institutions; in 1983 extension of the payment of family allowances to the first child, but at a lower rate and for a shorter period than for the second and subsequent children, together with an increase in the relative value of family allowances for the second child.

Despite the importance of these measures (whereby the share of financial allocations for family welfare as a percentage of total personal income more than doubled between 1966 and 1982), the main conclusions reached by the Hungarian specialists, based on the results of longitudinal studies of people who married in 1966, 1974 and 1982, was that these measures "could not influence significantly the final—completed—fertility level" but in fact exerted an impact on the incidence of births in the calender year in question; changes were reflected mainly in the shortening of the interval between the first and second children, and the lengthening of the interval between the second and third.[12] Nevertheless, it may be assumed that socialist countries which, within the context of global socio-economic planning, evolve sophisticated and integrated complex family policy measures could achieve—and have actually achieved—better results than most of the Western European countries.

Nevertheless, there are isolated examples of specific successes, where family policies have unequivocally achieved their goals. The goals, however, tend to be narrow ones, and the policies particularly strong. For example, Austria introduced compulsory medical supervision of mothers and babies, with the help of a "mother and child record book", in 1974. This involved paying substantial allowances to mothers who underwent medical examinations during pregnancy, and further allowances if the child underwent regular examinations during its first year of life. The policy was extremely effective, with the result that the infant mortality rate fell in Austria from 23 per thousand to 12 per thousand. Similar examples may also be found in France, where specific measures taken after the Second World War permitted a rapid decrease in the infant mortality rate from 47.4 per thousand in 1950 to 23.4 in 1964 and 8.3 in 1985, or in Romania, where the implementation of a vast programme of medical care for mothers and children resulted in a fall in the infant mortality rate from 116.7 per thousand in 1950 to 49.4 in 1970 and 25.6 in 1985. Of course, such measures have a positive effect on demographic trends as a whole, and thus deserved to be mentioned.

Another apparently explicable development is the rise in the birth rate in Czechoslovakia, which went up from 16.5 per thousand in 1971 to 19.5 in 1975—from being one of the lowest in Europe to the third highest. This certainly correlated with a great investment in family policies: Czechoslovakia increased family allowances and state-subsidised services such as day nurseries, reduced prices for families with children and developed special tax rebates. However, the age structure of the population was also changing, as were economic conditions, and the TFR dropped back from 2.43 in 1976 to 2.06 in 1985, nevertheless remaining among the highest in Europe (see table 1). It is difficult to conclude reliably that any or all of these policies were the actual cause of the rise in fertility in the 1970s. It is likely that they had some effect but unlikely that they provide the full explanation.

The experience of most European countries has been that family policies are not simple instruments with clear results. Declines in the birth rate in most countries have not been successfully counteracted, even where this was a specific objective. In some respects fertility seems to be cyclical: the birth rate declines, then increases and again declines. Whether or not this is the case, family policy still appears to be the reflection of a favourable political climate and, perhaps sometimes, an agent of change. It can help to encourage a trend: it rarely succeeds in reversing a trend.

Obviously one of the major factors in this field is the progress made in family-planning techniques. Thus, such factors as the desire of women to give birth at a preferred period of their lives have become more and more predominant as far as female reproductive behaviour is concerned.

It is clear that most family policies have not achieved pro-natalist goals. The number of large families has, as noted, declined despite, in many countries, family allowance systems that—at least in the past—paid more for the fourth child than for the first. Similarly, the growth in the number of one-parent families has occurred in most sections of society; some of these families depend largely on social security, while others do not. Furthermore, there has been a growth of one-parent families both in countries such as the United Kingdom, where just over half of lone mothers rely on social security, and in countries such as those in Eastern Europe, where most are in employment.

The lack of response (or the only temporary response) of demographic developments to family policy is in part a reflection of the complexity and multicausal nature of changes in modern, post-industrial societies. Changes in patterns of economic activity and in the availability of housing are almost certainly of much greater significance than changes in family allowances are likely to have been. It would seem that social security measures have been largely a response to, or an effect of, demographic and other changes in society rather than a cause.

This section has concentrated on the effects (largely unknown) of family policy on demographic change. In terms of the other objectives already discussed—alleviating poverty and redistributing income, providing choice, and influencing sex roles in the labour market—many countries can provide clearer evidence. But to review this would be beyond the scope of this study.

One of the main conclusions to be drawn from recent European experience in the field of social security related to family policies might be that a major influence, as far as fertility is concerned, is no doubt the effect of the prevailing social values in each country on individual behaviour; social legislation may therefore have a significant effect on demographic trends only in those countries where positive social values in favour of children and families are well developed and widespread among the population.

INDICATORS OF FUTURE CHANGE

Whether or not to support a family policy is no longer an issue of debate for the future. This is perhaps the first major achievement of the past few decades. Although in the present economic situation all forms of social security are under close scrutiny and are expected to demonstrate value for money, family support is one area on which there is a growing political consensus in Europe. The family is everywhere treated as a venerated institution, even though different governments may overtly or covertly adhere to different models. The issue is not whether to intervene, but why, how and at what level to intervene.

The commitment to family policy is based on the recognition of two facts. First, there is agreement that the young and the elderly require care and protection, and that it is a legitimate objective of societies and of governments to facilitate that care. The family, in its changing forms and functions, needs to be supported and enabled to provide that care, in partnership with the State.

Second, there is also a growing awareness that the times when families themselves are most in need of support are relatively short ones. The bearing and rearing of young children is increasingly taking place over shorter and shorter periods of family life. Table 15 gives an interesting illustration of this phenomenon. As a general trend, the percentage of women having their first child between 30 and 34 years is increasing in European countries, when compared with all women of the same age group giving birth to a child. At the same time, and still as a general trend, births to women aged 30–34 as a proportion of all births in the same year was decreasing in most countries (table 16). Two main conclusions could be derived from these figures: first, that fewer women desire to have a child after the age of 30; second, that among these women, a greater proportion will not have a second child. The combined effect of these two factors may be seen as one of the reasons for declining fertility rates.

Single parenthood, while growing rapidly, is also for many a stage between two two-parent family partnerships; at the same time, families will often be more fluid, with parents as well as children leaving home; social parenting will develop alongside biological parenting. Families will be trying to balance more labour market participation with the responsibilities of family life. When they finish caring for children, they may start caring for their dependent elderly. Some will experience periods of unemployment of one or both parents, and many more will be bringing up children in conditions of poverty.

Each of the demographic developments already discussed has implications which have yet to be fully appreciated in most countries.

Falling birth rates and smaller families suggest a new emphasis for social security policies. In the past these have focused on large families both because large families were (and still are) much more prone to poverty than small ones and because it was hoped that supporting large families would encourage population growth. Now there is evidence that

Table 15. Women in the age group 30–34 years giving birth to a first child, as a percentage of all women in the same age group giving birth to a child, 1963 and 1980 (or nearest year)

Country[1]	1963	1980
Austria	15.7	20.8
Belgium	15.0	22.5[2]
Bulgaria	12.7	17.8
Czechoslovakia	10.2	12.6[2]
Denmark	10.0	20.2
Finland	17.3	27.6
France	16.3	23.1
German Democratic Republic	10.2	13.9
Germany, Federal Republic of	19.2	29.4
Greece	26.3	25.4[3]
Hungary	14.9	18.6
Iceland	5.5	6.1
Ireland	12.8	12.4[4]
Italy	19.0	20.8[2]
Luxembourg	20.6	25.4
Netherlands	12.4	21.8[3]
Norway	13.8	20.4
Poland	11.5	12.2
Portugal	15.3	18.3[3]
Romania	17.5	12.4[5]
San Marino	19.7[6]	14.0[2]
Spain	15.1[7]	14.5[8]
Switzerland	21.0	28.1[3]
United Kingdom	21.0	28.1[9]
Yugoslavia	11.3	14.4[2, 10]
USSR	12.9[11]	11.1[12]
Byelorussian SSR	13.1[13]	12.2[7]
Ukrainian SSR	17.7[14]	16.0[15]

[1] No data available for Cyprus, Malta and Turkey. [2] Figures for 1978. [3] Figures for 1979. [4] Figures for 1977. [5] The figure for 1985 was 13.1. [6] Figures for 1964. [7] Figures for 1975. [8] Figures for 1976. [9] Figures for 1978–80. [10] The figure for 1982 was 17.2. [11] Figures for 1966. [12] Figures for 1974. [13] Figures for 1972. [14] Figures for 1973. [15] Figures for 1974.

Sources: United Nations: *Demographic Yearbooks*, 1969 and 1981 (New York); *Demografska statistika 1982* (Belgrade, 1986); *Anuarul Statistic al Republicii Socialiste Românica 1986* (Bucharest).

Table 16. Women in the age group 30–34 years giving birth to a child, as a percentage of all births in the same year, 1963 and 1980 (or nearest year)

Country[1]	1963	1980
Austria	18.5	14.2
Belgium	21.3	14.8[2]
Bulgaria	12.2	8.4
Cyprus	18.6	16.6
Czechoslovakia	13.8	11.3[2]
Denmark	15.3	18.9
Finland	18.1	23.1
France	21.4	19.9
German Democratic Republic	12.4	6.8
Germany, Federal Republic of	18.3	20.1
Greece	24.5	15.3
Hungary	13.6	10.5
Iceland	17.9	17.1
Ireland	26.5	23.8[3]
Italy	23.0	19.7[4]
Luxembourg	20.7	19.9
Malta	16.4[5]	20.5
Netherlands	23.3	20.5
Norway	19.0	18.8
Poland	18.5	13.7
Portugal	21.4	15.4[4]
Romania	14.3	10.8[6]
San Marino	22.1	15.2[4]
Spain	18.9[7]	19.9[8]
Sweden	19.4	23.7
Switzerland	20.8	23.3
United Kingdom	18.3	19.5[9]
Yugoslavia	17.4	11.6[2, 10]
USSR	18.0	13.1[11]

[1] No data available for Turkey. [2] Figures for 1978. [3] Figures for 1977. [4] Figures for 1979. [5] Figures for 1970. [6] The figure for 1985 was 13.3. [7] Figures for 1972. [8] Figures for 1976. [9] Figures for 1978–80. [10] The figure for 1982 was 10.4. [11] Figures for 1974.
Sources: As for table 15.

European member States, be it among governments, politicians, and employers' and workers' organisations.

Notes

[1] For further details on this classification, see S. Kamerman and A. Kahn (eds.): *Family policy: Governments and families in 14 countries* (New York, Columbia University Press, 1978).

[2] Although interesting but partial figures concerning EEC countries may be found in *Les politiques familiales des États membres de la Communauté européenne: modèles familiaux et législations sociales*, Documents COFACE (Brussels, Dec. 1987).

[3] International Social Security Association (ISSA): *Social security and family policy*, European Series, No. 8 (Geneva, 1983).

[4] N. Questiaux and J. Fournier: "France", in Kamerman and Kahn, op. cit., pp. 117–182.

[5] German Democratic Republic, Institute for Sociology and Social Policy, Academy of Sciences: *Demographic processes and population policies in the German Democratic Republic 1970–1984* (Berlin, n.d.).

[6] ILO: *Into the twenty-first century: The development of social security* (Geneva, 1984).

[7] ISSA: "Developments and trends in social security, 1984–1986", in *International Social Security Review* (Geneva, ISSA), 4/1986, p. 380.

[8] E. Borowczyk: "State social policy in favour of the family in East European countries", in *International Social Security Review*, 2/1986, p. 180.

[9] J. Bradshaw and D. Piachaud: *Child support in the European Community* (London, Bedford Square Press, 1980).

[10] J. Ermisch: *Impact of policy actions on the family and the household*, Discussion Paper No. 116 (London, Centre for Economic Policy Research, 1986).

[11] Hungarian Central Statistical Office, Demographic Research Institute: *The impact of policy measures other than family planning programmes on fertility*, Research Reports No. 18 (Budapest, 1984).

[12] ibid., p. 77.

INCOME MAINTENANCE FOR THE ELDERLY: THE INFLUENCE OF DEMOGRAPHIC CHANGE

3

The branch of social security concerned with disability, old-age and survivors' benefits is particularly sensitive to medium- and long-term changes in the age structure of the population. This branch, which is highly developed in Europe, includes national and occupational schemes covered by a body of legislation and made up of institutions constituting what is commonly referred to as a national "pension system".

The significant changes in fertility and mortality, and in the related demographic variables, observed in the recent past or forecast in various European countries, are fully described in Chapter 1. The purpose of this chapter is to analyse the impact of demographic trends on pension systems and to illustrate the situation prevailing in Europe, particularly as regards the cost and the "affordability" of a pension policy. Attention will be focused essentially on issues concerning public policy and the operation of national compulsory income maintenance schemes for the elderly based on legislation. Reference will be made when necessary to private occupational pension arrangements, whose scope has now reached considerable proportions in a number of Western European countries.[1]

After a brief reminder of the salient features of European pension systems having a bearing on demographic considerations, the following issues will be highlighted:

— the recent experience of European countries in dealing with the consequences of demographic change and rising pension expenditure;
— the specific influence of demographic factors on pension policy and costs;
— the relationship between demographic trends and the impact of other relevant economic or social parameters on pension policy and costs.

The chapter ends with a review of the options available to policy-makers. On the agenda for the future, the main question will be how to reconcile demographic trends with social, economic and financial considerations within a global and effective pension strategy.

NATURE AND SCOPE OF PENSION SYSTEMS IN EUROPE: A BRIEF OVERVIEW

Some European pension schemes date back to the end of the ninteenth century, while others have roots in legislation enacted at the beginning of the twentieth century. Contemporary pension provision is, however, the result of changes and new departures occurring mainly after the end of the Second World War. As a result of this process of evolution and adaptation, all European countries have now achieved a high standard of provision and show considerable similarity with regard to the overall objectives of pension policy and the scope of coverage in terms of the population covered. Where countries mainly differ is in the choice of means employed to achieve national pension objectives, such as the mix between public and private provision, the functions assigned to various tiers of pension coverage (basic protection, complementary benefits, etc.), the institutional pattern and the source of funds.

A full description of the nature and scope of European pension systems is not within the terms of reference of this book. Since the focus here is on the possible impact of demographic trends on the provision of pensions, it may be useful to recall the features of individual programmes that are more likely to respond to demographic change.

The first is the *extent of coverage* of the pension scheme, in terms of persons protected. Many countries have adopted broad-based national programmes covering all residents (called "universal" schemes). Examples are found in the Netherlands, Switzerland, the United Kingdom, and the Nordic countries. A very large system of solidarity between generations is thus established. Risks are largely pooled and the consequences of demographic change can be shared between all citizens.

In other countries pension schemes are organised separately for various socio-occupational groups. Many countries (e.g. Austria, France, Federal Republic of Germany, Italy and Spain), however, have one major "general" state pension scheme for employees, covering a large proportion of the working population, with the result that the pooling of risks and costs between people in various age groups is again very broad. In many Western European countries one finds that alongside the "general" scheme are "special" pension programmes or funds catering for specific occupational groups. Some may have a broad coverage (for instance, schemes covering persons employed in agriculture or a large section of the self-employed), but others may be limited to a specific occupational group (miners, railway workers, seafarers, etc.).

Most Eastern European countries follow the same pattern, designing "special" schemes for categories such as agricultural workers belonging or not belonging to the co-operative sector, or self-employed or handicraft workers. In some cases, however, similar categories are included in the framework of the "general" scheme, as for example in Hungary.

Naturally special schemes operate on a more limited pooling of risks, which makes them more vulnerable to changes in the ratio between working and retired members. When employment declines sharply and steadily over the years because of structural changes occurring in the economy, the proportionate increase in retired members will inevitably bring about or compound the financial imbalance of the pension fund.

The same observation could be made in respect of complementary or occupational pension funds established for the purpose of obtaining upon retirement a level of income better related to pre-retirement earnings.

In Western Europe these so-called "second-tier" programmes are either made compulsory for specific occupational groups by virtue of legislation, or left to be negotiated freely between employers and workers, within guide-lines and safeguards established by a supervisory state authority.

The first option, adopted, for instance, in the Nordic countries or in France (complementary pension schemes), generates schemes with a very broad coverage and pooling of risks.

The second option, on the contrary, leads to the establishment of "company pension funds" whose membership is limited to the employees of the company. The most significant examples can be found in the Federal Republic of Germany, the Netherlands, the United Kingdom, and the Nordic countries. In Switzerland the establishment, at the level of individual enterprises, of a complementary pension arrangement for employees has actually been made compulsory by recent legislation. In order to avoid the risk of financial instability, such as may result from demographic changes, these "enterprise-based" arrangements lacking a large pooling of risks operate under financial conditions (funding of future liabilities, re-insurance, etc.) that are different from those of other types of scheme.

In Eastern European countries examples of complementary occupational pension funds may be found in the German Democratic Republic and Romania. In both countries the funds were established on a voluntary basis for workers incorporated in the general pension schemes. However, since in Romania almost all workers became members of the voluntary occupational pension fund, the fund was made compulsory in

1985, thus becoming a kind of second tier of the general scheme, with the notable difference that the complementary scheme is financed only by workers' contributions. Although the voluntary scheme in the German Democratic Republic is becoming similarly generalised, it is not envisaged for the time being to make it compulsory. The USSR also introduced by law in 1987 the possibility for employees to take out voluntary complementary retirement plans with state insurance companies.

The second feature of a pension scheme worth recalling in the context of this discussion is the prevailing *financial organisation* of the pension system in the country concerned. In Europe the degree to which pensions are financed from employers' or employees' contributions or from general revenue varies considerably from one country to another, as shown by the examples in table 17.

There are also differences in the financial systems adopted, although the so-called "pay-as-you-go" method is generally applied, with minor variations, by either the universal programmes or the large "general" schemes protecting the majority of employed or self-employed persons.

Table 17. Composition of total receipts of social security pension schemes in selected European countries, 1983 (in percentages)

Subregion/country	Contributions from		Tax-financed state participation	Income from capital	Other income	Total income
	Insured persons	Employers				
Eastern Europe						
Czechoslovakia[1]	—	3.7	94.6	—	1.7	100
German Democratic Republic[1]	23.1	29.5	47.3	—	0.1	100
Hungary[1]	19.1	60.5	20.4	—	—	100
Romania[1,2]	—	100.0	—	—	—	100
USSR[1]	—	—	97.2[7]	—	2.8	100
Northern Europe						
Denmark[3]	3.1	3.7	84.6	8.6	—	100
Finland	11.9	57.4	14.7	15.9	0.1	100
Ireland[1]	23.4	48.7	27.7	0.1	0.1	100
Norway[1,4]	31.5	45.7	22.6	0.1	0.1	100
Sweden[3]	2.1	61.7	11.6	24.6	—	100
United Kingdom[1]	39.0	43.8	13.3	2.6	1.3	100

Table 17. (cont.)

Subregion/country	Contributions from		Tax-financed state participation	Income from capital	Other income	Total income
	Insured persons	Employers				
Southern Europe						
Cyprus[1]	35.1	35.4	20.6	8.1	0.8	100
Greece[1]	35.4	34.6	21.2	6.5	2.3	100
Italy[1]	12.0	53.8	32.3	0.8	1.1	100
Malta[1]	36.8	29.8	33.4	—	—	100
Portugal[1]	28.1	64.1	7.8	—	—	100
San Marino	27.6	42.1	30.3	—	—	100
Spain[1,5]	36.9	39.9	5.1	17.6	0.5	100
Turkey[1,4]	20.0	59.1	19.1	0.1	1.7	100
Yugoslavia[6]	66.7	23.0	9.7	0.1	0.5	100
Western Europe						
Austria[4]	33.8	34.3	29.6	0.3	2.0	100
Belgium[4]	34.6	41.5	20.4	3.3	0.2	100
Germany, Fed. Rep. of[3,4]	40.2	37.2	21.3	0.7	0.6	100
Luxembourg	31.3	26.4	23.7	14.9	3.7	100
Netherlands[1]	50.1	26.6	12.9	5.9	4.5	100
Switzerland	39.0	32.0	26.3	2.5	0.2	100

[1] Includes all social insurance schemes. [2] Without complementary pensions. [3] Includes supplementary pensions. [4] Without public employees' pensions. [5] Without unemployment benefits. [6] Pension insurance. [7] Represents payments from the State, state enterprises and state organisations which are fully included in the state budget.

Source: ILO: *The Cost of Social Security: Twelfth International Inquiry 1981–83*, Basic tables (Geneva, 1989).

As explained before, funding future liabilities (wholly or partially) is typical only of complementary (occupational) pension funds with limited membership.

A "pay-as-you-go" system means that the productive population of today has to provide (through contributions or taxation) the resources required to cover the current cost of pensions, while future generations will have to finance the pensions of those who are working today. An inter-generational transfer of financial responsibility thus takes place. In other words, the contribution or tax paid to the pension system by the workers does not pay for the cost of the pension "promise" which is currently made to them. Therefore a change in the age structure of the population, in the direction of further "ageing", represents—under a pay-as-you-go system of financing pensions—an undesirable threat to both workers and pensioners.

The mechanisms adopted to adjust pensions in course of payment to fluctuations in the overall level of wages, or more generally in the cost of living, also vary from country to country. Whether the protection of the purchasing power of pensioners is achieved through automatic indexation of pensions or a discretionary decision to raise them, it is obvious that policies adopted in this area will ultimately respond to cost considerations influenced, inter alia, by demographic factors.

The third important parameter to be considered is *pensionable age*, that is, the age at which an old-age pension is payable under social security legislation. The criteria adopted to determine pensionable age, whether or not they are flexible, have a major impact on the cost of a pension scheme. Demographic considerations should normally play a role in fixing or revising the pensionable age, but there are reasons to believe that in the past other considerations (e.g. financial or social) have prevailed.

A striking feature is that in Europe, once pensionable age is determined, it tends to remain unchanged for a very long period. In the Federal Republic of Germany the normal age of retirement (65 years) in the general scheme for employees dates back to 1916. In the USSR the retirement age of 60 for men and 55 for women has remained unchanged since the 1920s.

Similar examples can be found in Italy, where the present age limits (60 for men and 55 for women) were fixed in 1939, Spain, Sweden and some Eastern European countries.

However, there are also examples of European countries which have deliberately changed the statutory pensionable age from time to time. In Switzerland the AVS national pension for all residents, first legislated in 1946, provided an old-age pension at age 65 for men and women. In 1957 the age for women was lowered to 63 and then to 62 in 1964. In Denmark the basic mean-tested old-age pension introduced in 1933 was first paid at age 65 for men and at 60 for women. In 1967 these ages were raised to 67 for men and married women and 62 years for unmarried women. In 1984 the pensionable age for unmarried women was brought up to 67. More recently, a scheme allowing for the provision of partial pensions took effect in 1987. This applies to workers aged 60 to 67 and relates to both the universal scheme and to the occupational statutory complementary scheme (ATP). For the latter, applicants must have worked full time during at least ten years out of the last 20, and during nine months out of the last 12. In Norway the normal pensionable age (the basic pension for residents) was lowered from 70 to 67 in 1973.

In France a reduction from age 65 to age 60 of the minimum age for which a full old-age pension is due to employees in the "general" employees' scheme was legislated in 1981. In 1988 partial pension provisions were introduced, which enabled workers aged 60 and over having completed a full insurance career (150 quarters) to work on a part-time basis while drawing part of their pension rights from the basic scheme, as well as from the relevant statutory complementary pension scheme.

These provisions are akin to those made in Sweden in 1976, when the normal age for both the universal (basic) pension and the earnings-related pension was lowered from 67 to 65, at the same time as partial pensions were first introduced. Without altering the normal retirement age, Finland introduced in 1986 provisions for early retirement under the National Pension Plan, as well as within both the statutory and the voluntary supplementary pension schemes. In 1987 a part-time pension was introduced under the statutory supplementary pension scheme.

Thus, the most significant trend in the past decade has in fact been towards allowing greater "flexibility" in retirement age, by adopting a set of new eligibility conditions enabling persons to retire earlier than the "normal" statutory age (with or without a reduction in benefit), to postpone retirement (with or without an increase in benefit), or again to claim a partial pension.

It is not entirely clear whether increased flexibility in this area was motivated mainly or exclusively by labour market or social considerations, or whether demographic concern played a role. It would seem, however, unlikely that in the face of emerging demographic trends one could justify lowering the retirement age or making conditions more flexible in the direction of early retirement. It should also be recalled that flexibility with regard to pensionable age is not an entirely new feature in European social security legislation: it has long been practised in many countries in order either to take into consideration periods of employment spent in hazardous and unhealthy occupations, to give incentives to those who wish to work beyond retirement age or to award recognition to long service as such.

Many examples of this approach may be found in the legislation of the USSR and other centrally planned economy countries. Provisions enabling mothers who have reared a given number of children to retire before the "normal" age are more directly linked with demographic considerations. Such examples may be found, inter alia, in France and Romania (in both cases, for working mothers with at least three children).

Table 18. Pensionable age and flexible retirement provisions under state pension schemes, 1986

Country	Normal pensionable age		General provisions to make retirement flexible[1]	Specific provisions to make retirement flexible[2]
	Men	Women		
Austria	65	60	No	Yes
Belgium	65	60	Yes	No
Bulgaria	60	55	Yes	Yes
Cyprus	65	65	No	Yes
Czechoslovakia	60	53–57	No	Yes
Denmark	67	67	Yes	No
Finland	65	65	Yes	No
France	60	60	No	Yes
German Democratic Republic	65	60	No	Yes
Germany, Fed. Rep. of	65	65	Yes	No
Greece	65	60	Yes	Yes
Hungary	60	55	Yes	Yes
Iceland	67	67	No	No
Ireland	66	66	No	No
Italy	60	55	No	Yes
Luxembourg	65	65	No	Yes
Malta	61	60	No	No
Netherlands	65	65	No	No
Norway	67	67	Yes	No
Poland	65	60	Yes	Yes
Portugal	65	62	Yes	No
Romania	60	55	Yes	Yes
San Marino	60	55	No	No
Spain	65	65	No	Yes
Sweden	65	65	Yes	Yes
Switzerland	65	62	No	No
Turkey	55	50	No	Yes
United Kingdom	65	60	No	No
Yugoslavia	60	55	No	Yes
USSR	60	55	No	Yes

Table 18 summarises the present situation with regard to the statutory age of retirement in European countries.

THE INFLUENCE OF DEMOGRAPHIC CHANGES ON PENSION POLICY AND THE RESPONSE AT NATIONAL LEVEL

Concern about rising social security expenditure in Europe resulting from the gradual increase of the proportion of the elderly in the total population, or as a percentage of the population of working age, dates back several decades. Already in the 1950s governments studying the future development of pension expenditure realised that long-term trends of declining fertility and increasing longevity would eventually lead to considerably higher pension costs. For instance, the Phillips Committee appointed in 1953 in the United Kingdom—aware of the long-term implications of demographic trends—recommended that the statutory pensionable age should be gradually increased by three years. At that time the short-term outlook appeared more favourable because of the demographic effect of the so-called "baby boom" which most European countries experienced after the Second World War.

Specialists generally agree, therefore, that the unfavourable effect on social security of the ageing of European populations (with a few exceptions) has been statistically perceivable and predictable since the 1950s.

However, concern about demographic trends was not reflected in subsequent government policy on pensions, at least in the majority of the countries of Europe for which information is available. During the period when economic growth was sustained, most countries expanded social security coverage and improved benefits, in particular with regard to pensions. The methods available to protect pensioners against the erosion of their purchasing power in times of inflation were refined and made more responsive to individual needs. Retirement became more attractive because many older workers in Europe were more able to afford it.

Moreover, relatively sound economies and the slowly changing situation on the labour market made it acceptable to respond to social concern and to phase in early retirement provisions for special groups of

---

Notes to Table 18

[1] General flexibility means that legislation provides a measure of choice for *all* insured persons to advance or postpone pensionable age within the limits and under the conditions stipulated by law. [2] Specific flexibility means that legislation provides for more favourable conditions as regards pensionable age only in respect of specific categories of insured workers prescribed by law (i.e. those who have worked in unhealthy or hazardous occupations, or who belong to prescribed types of occupation).

Source: United States, Department of Health and Human Services: *Social security programs throughout the world, 1985* (Washington, DC, 1986).

workers such as the disabled, the unemployed and those in arduous employment. As described above, various flexible or early retirement provisions, which both had the same effect, namely to lower the average retirement age, began to emerge in the late 1960s and early 1970s. In many countries these are now more or less explicitly designed to combat unemployment or to ease the financial problems of the elderly unemployed.

As a result the actual age (as opposed to the statutory age) of retirement effectively declined in a number of countries, as shown in table 19. These data clearly confirm the constant trend, already shown in previous studies,[2] towards the use of flexible retirement provisions by workers, when these appear to be attractive enough.

The onset of the economic recession in the mid-seventies and the subsequent events, such as the apparently intractable problem of the growing number of unemployed workers, shook the complacency with which many people viewed the future during the earlier years of steady economic growth. The threat posed by the ageing of the population in practically all European countries was analysed more systematically by governments and the social partners. Public opinion thus became aware of the implications of demography on the financing of pensions in future years.

Yet at the same time, many workers were, as shown above, still retiring earlier, which meant that the ratio of pensioners to employed persons increased further. In some countries the right to retire early was granted with the aim of releasing jobs for younger people. This approach added further to the current and future cost of pensions.

Before reviewing national experience, it may be useful to recall that the ILO did not fail to draw attention to the emerging issues and to contribute from an international viewpoint to the current debate on pension policy and the position of the elderly. As shown in studies published by the ILO over the past ten years,[3] and from information it has gathered recently, several governments and the social partners were led to reassess the financial outlook of the pension system and to consider the adoption of possible remedial measures—although whether or not concern over demographic prospects was the major motivation for the action taken remains an open question. However, there is no doubt that it contributed to the awareness that pension policy should be reassessed without further delay.

The challenge was taken up by a number of Western European countries, which in the 1980s embarked upon major reforms of their pension systems.

A very thorough review of the social security system was put in hand in 1983 in the *United Kingdom*. In view of the broad scope of the studies

Table 19. Actual average retirement age in selected European countries, 1960–83/84 (in years)

Country	1960	1965	1970	1975	1980	1983/84
Austria						
Male	64.6	62.9	62.6	62.9	61.6	61.3[4]
Female	60.1	60.0	61.1	60.4	58.7	58.6[4]
Germany,[1] *Fed. Rep. of*						
(*a*) Manual workers' scheme						
Male	58.8	60.9	61.1	60.6	57.9	58.1[5]
Female	59.0	61.0	61.6	61.6	60.0	60.4[5]
(*b*) Non-manual workers' scheme						
Male	61.6	62.8	62.8	62.5	60.5	60.4[5]
Female	58.1	59.9	60.6	60.5	59.5	59.6[5]
France[2]						
Employed persons' scheme						
Male	—	—	—	—	63.3	62.3[5]
Female	—	—	—	—	63.5	62.6[5]
Total	—	63.9	64.0	63.6	63.4	62.4[5]
Hungary						
Male	—	—	—	61.7	60.6	60.6[5]
Female	—	—	—	57.3	56.8	56.4[5]
Luxembourg[3]						
(*a*) Manual workers' scheme						
Male	63.1	62.7	63.0	63.7	62.6	61.8[4]
Female	66.2	65.7	65.2	71.2	64.4	63.9[4]
(*b*) Non-manual workers' scheme						
Male	64.3	64.0	63.8	64.2	62.4	62.4[4]
Female	65.6	64.1	63.7	69.4	64.0	62.0[4]

[1] All pension awards except survivors' pensions. [2] Pensions excluding survivors' pensions (*droits directs*). [3] Old-age and early retirement pensions only. [4] Figures for 1983. [5] Figures for 1984.

Sources: Austria—R. Holzmann: *Issues in the development of public pension schemes: International and historical perspectives*, Paper No. 7, given at the Joint Japanese/OECD Conference of High-Level Experts on Health and Pension Policies in the Context of Demographic Evolution and Economic Constraint, Tokyo, November 1985; Federal Republic of Germany—data supplied directly by the Federal Ministry of Labour; France—various issues of *Statistiques* or *Recueil statistique*, published by the Caisse nationale d'assurance vieillesse des travailleurs salariés; Hungary—Centre national d' études supérieures de sécurité sociale: *L'impact de la crise sur la sécurité sociale 1974–1984, Hongrie*, Research report for the ILO (Paris, 1986); Luxembourg–ministère de la Sécurité sociale: *Rapport général sur la sécurité sociale au Grand-duché de Luxembourg*.

and proposals made, and the fact that new legislation was finally adopted in 1986, it is worth describing the relevant experience in some detail. Before the reform, the state pension scheme in the United Kingdom was made up of two tiers: a universal flat-rate benefit, introduced in 1948, and a wage-related component (the state earnings-related pension scheme—SERPS), built up as from 1975. (Employers were, however, able to "contract out" of SERPS as long as the benefits provided under the alternative scheme were not lower than those of SERPS.) The country faced the prospect of major increases in the cost of retirement benefits due to the rise in the real value of pensions, the increasing maturity of the system and, above all, the forecast increase in the proportion of the elderly within the total population. It was thus obvious that reform was necessary.

The reform aimed at promoting long-term measures which would contain the increase in the future cost of state pensions. These measures, however, could not be applied at once, as a transition period had been deemed necessary. Another objective was to reduce the involvement of the State in the provision of wage-related pensions, by giving all workers the opportunity to make their own arrangements for personal pensions with private financial organisations, if they so desired.

One of the main results was the reform of SERPS. Although the wage-related component was not abolished, and the "contracting out" provisions were maintained, its benefits were substantially curtailed in order to obtain, in the long run, an overall cost saving estimated at 25 per cent. Measures taken include a phased-in reduction of SERPS benefit levels from 25 to 20 per cent of wages, a requirement that such benefits should be related to wages received throughout the whole working life (and not only the best 20 years) and the reduction of entitlements for surviving spouses of insured persons.

As a counterpart to the reduction in the state commitment towards pensions, incentives have been given for the establishment of personal pensions. From 1988 individuals can make their own pension arrangements, opting out of SERPS or the employer's occupational pension scheme if they wish to do so. Those opting out will benefit from a 2 per cent rebate on earnings between the lower and upper limits subject to national insurance contributions (with a minimum of £1 per week) during fiscal years 1988/89 to 1992/93. Occupational schemes will also have to allow members to make additional voluntary contributions if they wish to do so and to give employees leaving a job before retirement age a refund of their contributions if they have less than two years' membership of a scheme. Personal pensions will have to be approved by the Occupational Pensions Board.

Although the Bill came into force on 1 April 1988, the changes to

SERPS will not affect anyone retiring this century. There will be a ten-year transitional period from the year 2000, before the new scheme comes fully into effect in 2010.

In *Austria* a reappraisal of the state pension programme for employees led to changes in the eligibility conditions effective from January 1985. From January 1987 pensions are based on the earnings of the last ten years prior to retirement instead of the last five before 1985, seven in 1985 and nine in 1986. The basic pension of 30 per cent of the reference earnings for the first ten contribution years—justified 30 years ago to favour workers with short insurance records—was abolished; the amount of pensions was made almost linearly dependent upon the number of contribution years. Furthermore, the level of unemployment will in future be taken into account when deciding on the annual adjustment of pensions in line with the cost of living. These measures are intended to contain the future expenditure on benefits.

Belgium considerably reduced differences in eligibility conditions and methods of calculating pensions between the schemes for civil servants, employees and the self-employed through harmonisation legislation which came into effect in June 1984. At the same time the Government introduced cost-containment measures, such as a ceiling on the maximum pension, a limitation of the possibility of freely accumulating pensions from different sources and a slowing down of the indexation of current pensions; the latter meant that the so-called "welfare coefficient", which linked increases in pensions to the development of the national wealth, was no longer taken into account.

The Government acknowledged in 1985 that, in the light of future demographic developments, other long-term adjustments in pensions might be necessary. However, efforts by the Government to raise the retirement age for women from 60 to 65 seem to have failed, in view of objections raised by workers' and employers' associations when the National Labour Council met in January 1987. The final outcome of the Council is awaited.

In 1984 *Denmark* adopted a significant reform of the pension system covering all residents, in order to eliminate, among other things, differential treatment between men and women. While the entitlement to a pension before the normal retirement age had previously been regulated by ten different laws, as from 1984 there are only three categories of early retirement and disability benefits. The pensionable age for unmarried women was raised from 62 to 67. Widows' benefits were abolished, because according to the new enactments all women are entitled to early retirement pensions in their own right.

The report published jointly in 1985 by the Danish Council of Trade Unions and the major opposition party might be seen as an indirect reaction to those measures. This report recommended as from 1989 the introduction of a new statutory complementary scheme to supersede the existing one which provides only flat-rate benefits. The benefits of the new fund would be calculated on the basis of the wage-related contributions actually paid by employers and employees. During the first 12 years of the scheme, however, flat-rate benefits would still be maintained.

With explicit reference to the different demographic outlooks of the four individual national pension schemes (the manual workers' scheme, the private employees' scheme, the pension scheme for workers in small craft industries and commerce and the agricultural pension scheme), *Luxembourg* opted in 1985 for reviewing the financing rather than the benefit provisions. A global contribution rate applying to all schemes and calculated to remain stable for periods of seven years generated a common reserve fund of 1.5 to 2.5 times the expected annual expenditure. Each month the overall revenue is allocated to the different funds, thus enabling them to cover their expenditure.

In the *Netherlands* containment of the growth in the statutory minimum wage lowered the linked social security benefits, notably pensions, by 9 per cent in real terms between 1983 and 1986. These measures were obviously regarded as first steps towards a more general reform of the social security system.

In 1985 the Scientific Council for Government Policy in the Netherlands made a proposal for a radical restructuring of the complex system of cash benefits for disability, sickness, unemployment and old age. The existing set of entitlements was replaced by a new benefit structure including:

(a) a basic income guarantee, financed by taxation and available to all residents, at different rates according to category (the aged, widows, the permanently handicapped, the unemployed, etc.), to be increased, if necessary, by means-tested assistance;

(b) a benefit against loss of income payable to employees and the self-employed, which would supplement the basic income guarantee (financed by contributory social insurance);

(c) a private complementary benefit scheme open on a voluntary basis to those who aim at a level of protection above that offered by the state programmes.

It appears that the aim of the proposal is that of restricting compulsory social security protection to a level of benefit considered to be a reasonable minimum.

In *Spain* a gradual process to reform the social security system is under way. Its aims are manifold: modernisation and updating of obsolete legislation; rationalisation of national pension programmes;

reduction, if possible, of emerging financial imbalances; adoption of more equitable benefits; and encouragement of private occupational pensions. The first stage of the reform was completed with an Act, passed in July 1985, providing for the integration of a number of special pension schemes covering different groups of employees into the general scheme. The Act also includes a series of restrictive measures: more stringent qualifying conditions for the receipt of pensions, particularly concerning the length of the required period of paid-up contributions, which has been raised from ten to 15 years; and modifications to the base used for calculating pensions, leading to an ultimate reduction in their levels. In exchange, the legislation introduced a provision for automatic annual indexation of pensions to prices.

In *Switzerland* an Act making second-tier occupational pensions mandatory for all wage earners and voluntary for the self-employed entered into force on 1 January 1985. These private occupational pension schemes are financed by employers' and employees' contributions and are fully funded. A security fund, mutually financed from the income of occupational pension funds, guarantees the payment of benefits should an unfavourable age structure of the membership of the fund—or bankruptcy of the employer—affect the solvency of the mandatory arrangements. More recently proposals have been advanced concerning the possible increase of pensionable age for women under the universal AVS basic pension scheme for all residents. The age limit for women is now 62, while men are entitled to an AVS pension at age 65.

In many other European market economy countries the pension system has been reassessed, although major or specific changes have not taken place so far.

In *France* a government commission was set up in 1985 to analyse the long-term cost outlook of the pension schemes beyond 2005. The report of the commission suggests:

— a fair and equitable distribution of the additional future costs between economically active and retired persons by a combination of higher contributions, gradually decreasing income replacement rates and a higher pensionable age, if economically feasible;

— a clarification of the role and scope of state pension provision by emphasising the traditional social insurance mechanism;

— a fair distribution of costs between members of different pension schemes where economic and demographic conditions are not the same. In other words, it is desirable to harmonise benefits and contributions within a wider concept of pooling of risks.[4]

In 1987 a report of a special committee to the Government *(Comité des Sages)* suggested a progressive increase in the normal retirement age, and the basing of the average wage for pension entitlement on the best 20 or 25 years, instead of ten.

In the *Federal Republic of Germany* a general structural reform of the retirement system is envisaged for the late 1980s or early 1990s. So far, the Government has issued only basic principles for the planned reform, which should aim at keeping the earnings-related benefit system unchanged, at encouraging private provisions for old age and at achieving an equitable distribution of the future financial burden between active and retired persons, e.g. by avoiding increases in pensions greater than the disposable income of contributors.

Paradoxically, one additional step towards improving the financial balance of pension funds is to be found in provisions effective from January 1983 and related to the financing of health care for pensioners. Up until that date, the cost of these measures was supported by the pension funds, which paid to the various health insurance funds amounts calculated on the same basis as the contributions for active members. The reform introduced a financial commitment for pensioners to contribute personally out of their pensions to the health funds at a rate gradually reaching one-half of the global 11.7 per cent. The whole operation has resulted in an increase of the financial resources of pension funds devoted to the actual payment of long-term benefits, through an indirect increased contribution by pensioners.

As a final example of the current changes in the Federal Republic of Germany to ensure that social security is on a sound financial footing, new legislation which took effect in January 1987 requires employers to set up book reserves according to precise provisions for any private pension promise made after 31 December 1986.

In *Italy* pension reform has been on the Government's agenda for several years. At the beginning of 1987, following an initiative taken directly by Parliament, proposals for reform appeared to be closer to obtaining agreement from the parties concerned. The main changes under discussion include:

(a) raising the retirement age gradually (at present 55 for women and 60 for men) having due regard to the need for flexibility;

(b) imposing a ceiling on earnings subject to pension contributions in order to gradually free personal and corporate income as an incentive to establish complementary occupational pension arrangements (still very rare in Italy);

(c) tightening the eligibility conditions by raising from 15 to 20 the minimum number of years required for old-age pension entitlement; and

(d) shifting to general-revenue financing part of the welfare expenditure now unduly borne by the contributory scheme for employed persons.

In *Norway* awareness of the future increase in pension expenditure has grown in recent years. This has led to a general perception that there is no more room for further improvements in benefits. The Ministry of Social Affairs commissioned a comprehensive report outlining the various options open to the country for possible adjustment and reform of the pension scheme. The resulting study[5] was presented by the Minister as aiming to stimulate the social policy debate on pensions.

In Eastern European countries pension policy planners are dealing with a somewhat different situation. First, there are still regional shortages in the supply of labour (as in the USSR) and consequently pension incentives are not used to induce workers to retire earlier, but rather to reward those who stay at work beyond normal retirement age. Second, the statutory retirement age tends to be lower, on average, than in Western Europe. Third, economic activity rates are higher at all ages and therefore the ratios of pensioners to working population are more favourable.

The consequence of all these factors is a different attitude towards the future impact on pensions of emerging changes in the age structure of the population.

More specifically, pension planners are now searching for a more "dynamic" pension formula in order to improve the level of benefits in response to changes in the general level of wages and consumer prices. This subject is now under discussion, for instance, in *Czechoslovakia* and in *Bulgaria*, where changes are planned.

In *Hungary* changes in the pension system might include an increase from ten to 20 years of the minimum period of insurance qualifying for a pension, the adoption of flexible retirement provisions (including incentives to postpone retirement), the introduction of a ceiling on contributions and benefits and an improved method of adjusting pensions to keep pace with changes in the cost of living.

In the *USSR* it was recently decided to carry out an overall review of pension provisions. One area of study is the system of incentives (through wages or pension measures) to encourage workers to postpone their age of retirement. It was reported that, at present, about 60 per cent of pensioners remain in the workplace after drawing their old-age pension, and that on average they go on working for another five or six years. The rules concerning compatibility between pensions and wage income in such cases are under review.

Another set of issues under discussion in the USSR concerns the special provisions which allow workers engaged in unhealthy or arduous occupations to draw an old-age pension up to ten years before attaining the normal age. However, such preferential treatment is conditional on working in a prescribed occupation which appears on a list dating back to 1956. Because of changes in conditions of work and technology, it is believed that many of the prescribed occupations are no longer arduous or unhealthy. The solution envisaged in the USSR might introduce more flexible criteria for an early pension, following perhaps the example of Romania and Yugoslavia where, apart from a very restricted number of prescribed occupations, the test of unhealthy or arduous work depends on the job actually performed by the individual worker during his or her career. The relevant rules are also being reviewed in Yugoslavia for the purpose of unifying the criteria applied in different republics and territories.

The situation regarding pension rights in *Yugoslavia* is as follows: since 1983 pensions have been determined by the monthly average personal income earned by the insured person in any of the ten consecutive years of insurance most favourable to him or her. From 1987 personal incomes earned in previous years will be gradually calculated on the basis of income earned in the last year of working life. The full application of this system should begin in 1990. A possible reduction of the number of years of economic activity required for entitlement to an old-age pension is being considered in view of the pressing problems of high unemployment of young professionals.

The few examples quoted above show that demographic evolution in the USSR and in Eastern Europe is not seen at the moment as a major threat to the financial position of the State pension schemes. Czechoslovakia, the German Democratic Republic and Romania, for instance, have indicated that pension financing will continue to be taken care of under successive five-year plans by an appropriate allocation of resources, either from general revenue or from levies on enterprises (as, for instance, in Romania).

PAST TRENDS IN PENSION EXPENDITURE AND ITS "DEMOGRAPHIC" COMPONENT

Before we turn to the prospects for the future, particularly as regards the effect of demographic and related trends, two questions deserve to be put briefly into perspective:
— the medium- and long-term trends of pension expenditure; and
— the share of rising costs that can be attributed to demographic factors alone.

For social security planners both questions, particularly the second one, may be of considerable importance. This is because the growth in the cost of maintaining the elderly, and the question of the "afford-ability" of a given pension policy, is linked to many factors, *of which demography is only one.*

International comparisons inevitably encounter the crucial problems of compatibility and comparability of data. Absolute figures are less comparable than the trends which emerge from their changes over time.

Tables 20 and 21 set out two key indicators of the past financial trends of national pension schemes in Europe. The indicators chosen here are (*a*) the time series of pension expenditure measured as a share of the gross domestic product (GDP) for the industrialised market economy countries, or as a share of the net material product (NMP) for the centrally planned economy countries, and (*b*) the indicator of the "real" (price-adjusted) absolute growth of pension expenditure. These two sets of figures were selected because they can be regarded as describing in a nutshell the cost of state pensions in a given national context.

The figures shown in tables 20 and 21 suggest the following. The first half of the 1970s was a period of fast growth in pension expenditure in the majority of European countries. As explained earlier, during that period the commitment of the State towards the elderly and the disabled was enlarged: coverage was extended and benefits improved. During the second half of the decade the growth of pension expenditure slowed down in a number of countries, probably as a result of cost-containment policies which began to be applied, and the fact that within several programmes insured persons were earning more and more pension rights.

Beginning in 1980 the data indicate that in the majority of countries the share of pension expenditure in GDP tended to remain constant. There are a few exceptions (Austria, Greece, Italy, Malta) to this general trend, which seems otherwise to hold good for the various regions of Europe.

The days when the European economies could accommodate growth rates in their social security (pensions) outlay in excess of those of GDP or NMP seem to be over in a large number of countries. Pension expenditure as a proportion of GNP/NMP varied in 1983 between 5.8 per cent (United Kingdom) and 11.4 per cent (Netherlands). This range of values reflects differences in policy objectives and benefit structure, and in the demographic structure of the population. There may also be minor variations resulting from different statistical definitions in individual national accounting systems.

Since the demographic factor is known to be only one among others that are responsible for the past increase in pension expenditure, it is

Table 20. Pension expenditure[1] as a percentage of GDP,[2] 1970–83

Subregion/country	1970	1975	1980	1983
Eastern Europe				
Bulgaria	6.6	7.2	7.8	8.6
Czechoslovakia	8.0	7.8	9.9	10.8
German Democratic Republic	7.8	8.6	9.3	n.a.
Hungary	4.7	6.8	9.5	10.1
Poland	4.4	4.6	7.0	n.a.
Northern Europe				
Denmark	5.0	6.4	7.8	8.0
Finland	3.7	5.3	6.2	6.8
Ireland	3.0	4.5	5.3	6.2
Norway	5.9	7.1	7.5	7.8
Sweden	5.3	7.3	9.7	10.4
United Kingdom	4.0	5.4	5.6	5.8
Southern Europe				
Cyprus	1.3	2.8	2.2	n.a.
Greece	4.8	4.4	5.5	8.9
Italy	5.9	9.5	6.8[3]	8.8[3]
Malta	2.8	6.2[4]	6.1	7.4
Portugal	0.9	3.2	5.4	5.7
Spain	—	3.4	5.8	7.3
Turkey	0.4	0.3	1.4	1.7
Western Europe				
Austria	7.2	8.0	8.8	10.9
Belgium	4.2	5.8	6.5	7.0
France	4.3	6.9	7.7	9.5
Germany, Fed. Rep. of	6.8	8.4	9.4	9.7
Luxembourg	6.8	8.5	9.8	9.8
Netherlands	7.2	9.3	11.2	11.4
Switzerland	4.1	7.3	7.5	7.4
USSR	5.5	6.7	7.3	7.3

[1] Includes in some cases the expenditure of complementary schemes.   [2] In the USSR and in Eastern Europe the GDP is replaced by the NMP.   [3] Owing to reorganisation of the social security system the data are not compatible with previous ones.   [4] The national accounting system was changed.

Source: ILO: *The Cost of Social Security: Twelfth International Inquiry*, op. cit.

Table 21. Increase in real[1] aggregate pension[2] expenditure, 1975-83 (base year: 1970 = 100)

Subregion/country	1975	1980	1983
Eastern Europe			
Bulgaria	145	185	n.a.
Czechoslovakia	125	175	n.a.
Gèrman Democratic Republic	149	191	n.a.
Hungary	240	278	n.a.
Poland	165	260	n.a.
Northern Europe			
Denmark	151	213	n.a.
Finland	183	237	285
Ireland	207	296	352
Norway	150	201	219
Sweden	157	231	249
United Kingdom	145	182	218
Southern Europe			
Cyprus	163	254	n.a.
Greece	114	172	273
Italy	186	165	219
Malta	280	617	660
Portugal	280	860	n.a.
Spain	100[3]	182	n.a.
Turkey	107	598	n.a.
Western Europe			
Austria	136	175	225
Belgium	166	208	212
France	192	250	n.a.
Germany, Fed. Rep. of	138	185	183
Luxembourg	138	190	n.a.
Netherlands	156	223	220
Switzerland	188	209	214
USSR	150	200	214

[1] Expenditure adjusted by the respective national consumer price indices. [2] Includes in some cases the expenditure of complementary schemes. [3] The base year for Spain is 1975, as figures for pension expenditure are available only from that date.

Source: ILO: *The Cost of Social Security: Eleventh International Inquiry 1978–80*, (Geneva, 1985), and preliminary data of the *Twelfth International Inquiry*, op. cit.

interesting to refer here to a recent OECD study[6] which attempts to break down the overall rate of growth in pension expenditure into three components:

— the impact of the demographic factor;
— the effects of extending coverage;
— the consequences of improving benefits.

This study covers only the major European market economy countries. Its findings are shown in table 22.

Table 22 shows that, at least in the major market economy countries, the increase in average real benefits was the major determinant of the real increase in overall pension expenditure between 1960 and 1975, and even in the period of lower growth rates (1975–81). Demographic change was the second major source of expansion but far less important than the combined effect of improvements in benefits and extensions in coverage.

Apart from the OECD study referred to above, available information shows that there are good reasons to believe that the gradual increase in the average benefit paid to retired and disabled people is also an important factor influencing the overall growth of pension expenditure in other countries. This is the case in Poland, where the average real pension (i.e. adjusted for price changes) increased between 1970 and 1983 by 0.4 per cent per annum, or in Hungary, where the overall figure was +5.4 per cent for the same period.

Given the demographic evidence shown in Chapter 1, and the fact that most countries in Europe are likely to be showing restraint as far as benefits are concerned, future changes in the age composition of the population will probably have an increasing impact on the future real growth of pension expenditure.

THE RELATIONSHIP BETWEEN DEMOGRAPHIC AND ECONOMIC FACTORS INFLUENCING PENSION EXPENDITURE

The simplest way to break down into its components the cost of a pension scheme financed on a pay-as-you-go basis in order to better understand the role of demographic trends is to look separately at two ratios:

(a) the number of pensioners as a percentage of the number of the active members of the scheme (the "demographic rate");
(b) the average benefit as a percentage of the average earnings (income) of the members of the scheme (the "financial rate").

In the context of the financial analysis of pension schemes, it has long been demonstrated that under certain assumptions the product of the

Table 22. Breakdown of growth rates of pension expenditure in selected European countries (in percentages)

Country/ period	Real annual average growth rate of pension expenditure	Share attributable to:[1]		
		Demographic factors	Extension of coverage	Increase in average real benefits
Finland				
1960–75	11.1	2.8	0.04	8.0
1975–81	5.5	2.5	−0.5	3.4
France				
1960–75	7.7	1.9	1.9	3.7
1975–81	8.7	0.8	3.0	4.7
Germany, Fed. Rep. of				
1960–75	6.3	3.1	−0.3	3.4
1975–81	2.1	0.9	1.4	−0.2
Ireland				
1960–75	8.2	0.7	1.5	5.9
1975–81	6.6	1.1	0.7	4.7
Italy				
1960–75	9.6	2.6	0.3	6.5
1975–81	7.7	2.5	−2.9	8.2
Netherlands				
1960–75	10.3	2.7	−0.2	7.6
1975–81	5.2	2.0	0.4	2.7
Norway				
1960–75	12.1	2.1	2.8	6.8
1975–81	4.6	1.9	0.4	2.2
Sweden				
1960–75	8.7	2.3	0.2	6.0
1975–81	6.9	2.7	2.3	6.9
United Kingdom				
1960–75	5.9	1.6	0.9	3.3
1975–81	4.5	1.0	0.8	2.6

[1] The shares given here do not amount to a simple total of the real annual average growth rate, which was calculated using a complex methodology.

Source: OECD: *Social expenditure, 1960–1990* (Paris, 1985), Ch. 2.

demographic rate and the financial rate, as defined above, is an indicator of the average cost of the scheme in terms of a percentage of covered earnings.

This relationship is recalled here without further development simply to note that if one assumes that average benefits and insured earnings maintain approximately the same relationship over time, then a significant alteration of the number of elderly persons as compared with the number of persons of working age will directly influence the future cost of a pension scheme. Experience, however, shows that the so-called "financial rate" is far from being stable in the context of European schemes; for instance, in many countries average benefits will most probably continue to rise, as insured persons earn more and more entitlements and acquire additional years of insurance, residence or contributions. Moreover, the trends in average earnings are not easily predictable. We shall return later to the future outlook of the financial aspects.

Using the statistical data from Chapter 1, it has been possible to work out the future trend of the demographic component in Europe by using, first of all, an approximate indicator—the gross dependency ratio, i.e. the number of persons aged 60 and over as a percentage of those aged 20 to 59. Table 23 shows the values of this rate, as well as its expected increase, between 1985 and 2025. It can be seen that the gross dependency ratio is at present substantially lower in the USSR and in Eastern Europe than,

Table 23. Old-age gross dependency ratios in European subregions, 1985 and 2025

Subregion	Ratio of population aged 60 and over to population aged 20–59		
	1985	2025	% increase
Eastern Europe[1]	29.1	42.7	+46.7
Northern Europe[2]	39.3	51.4	+30.8
Southern Europe[3]	30.7	46.1	+50.2
Western Europe[4]	34.1	57.9	+69.8
USSR	24.0	41.3	+72.1

[1] Includes Bulgaria, Czechoslovakia, German Democratic Republic, Hungary, Poland, Romania. [2] Includes Denmark, Finland, Iceland, Ireland, Norway, Sweden, United Kingdom. [3] Includes Albania, Greece, Italy, Malta, Portugal, Spain, Yugoslavia. [4] Includes Austria, Belgium, France, Federal Republic of Germany, Luxembourg, Netherlands, Switzerland.

Source: ILO: *Economically active population: Estimates and projections, 1950–2025* (Geneva, 3rd ed., 1986).

for instance, in Northern and Western Europe. However, the expected increase in this ratio over the next 40 years would be more substantial in the USSR where, at present, the phenomenon of "ageing" is less evident.

The figures shown so far are not, however, sufficiently explicit or informative in the context of pension policy planning. The reason is that not all persons presumed to be active (on the basis of their age) are in gainful employment and not all those who are presumed to be old have retired from work or are drawing a pension. One must therefore examine the forecasts available as regards labour force participation rates, by age group, and consider the impact of the level of unemployment on future pension costs.

Trends and projections of labour force participation rates, by age group, are periodically established by the ILO. The last set of ILO projections was made in 1985. These show, according to given assumptions, the proportion of persons in a given age group who are counted as part of the labour force (although they may not necessarily be in gainful employment) as compared with the total population in the corresponding age bracket.

In past years labour force participation rates have changed considerably in Europe. The proportion of persons aged 55 or more who belonged to the labour force declined sharply between 1950 and 1985 in all European subregions (see table A.6 in the statistical appendix). The total for Europe declined from 51.2 per cent to 20.5 per cent. While activity rates for men over 55 decreased in all subregions, the rates for women followed the same trend, except, however, in Northern Europe.

The trend revealed by the figures on activity rates for the elderly can be explained. First, the growth of social security pension provision in Europe over the past decades has induced many people to retire from the labour force. As mentioned earlier, retirement has gradually become more "affordable". Second, many European market economy countries have introduced strong incentives in the recent past to encourage people to retire earlier, the motivation being the desire to adapt the size of the labour force to the declining demand for labour resulting from modernisation and structural changes in the economy.

Looking then to the future, two observations can be made.

The first is that reference to the economic activity rates provides a sharper measure of the likely future relationship between pensioners and active persons than that obtained by projecting total population data only, as was done in table 23. This is illustrated in table 24, which compares the gross dependency ratios from table 23 (population aged 60 and over/age group 20–59) with those using labour force data. The percentage increases between 1985 and 2025 are slightly higher in all subregions of Europe if the latter measure is used.

Table 24. Alternative forecasts of old-age gross dependency ratios in European subregions (percentage change between 1985 and 2025)

Subregion	Total population data	Labour force data
	60 and over	Non-active 60 and over
	20–59	Total active population
Eastern Europe	+46.7	+56.7
Northern Europe	+30.8	+36.3
Southern Europe	+50.2	+55.1
Western Europe	+69.8	+73.8
USSR	+72.1	+73.6

Source: ILO: *Economically active population . . .* , op. cit.

The second observation is that even the above forecasts are not entirely satisfactory from the standpoint of pension policy. In fact, persons statistically counted as belonging to the labour force may or may not be in gainful employment. The unemployed—whose numbers are at present considerable in many subregions of Europe—cannot be counted upon to support their contemporaries in retirement through the income transfers set in motion by social security. Moreover, not all the elderly counted in the projections as not belonging to the labour force are—or will be—in receipt of a state pension (full or reduced).

Forecasts should therefore be adjusted to take these factors into account as far as possible. Before doing so, however, it is worth looking again at the earlier forecasts (table 24) and assuming, for the sake of argument, that activity rates for the elderly (aged 60 and over), males and females, had remained and would remain constant at the level observed in 1960, that is, broadly before the early retirement incentives became significant in the market economy countries of Northern, Southern and Western Europe. For these subregions a revised forecast (B) is shown in table 25 and compared with that given earlier (A).

As already said, the decrease in the economic activity rates was due to a combination of two factors: improved pension arrangements, on the one hand, and higher unemployment, on the other. This, of course, leads to a kind of blurring of the influence of demographic factors *per se*. Thus if the activity rates observed in 1960 for persons aged 60 and over continued to apply in 1985—and if they were to remain unchanged until 2025—then the actual increase in the dependency ratio solely due to the

Table 25. Alternative forecasts of the increase in the proportion of non-active persons aged 60 and over to the total active population[1]

Subregion		Ratio of non-active persons aged 60 and over to active population		% change, 1985–2025
		1985	2025	
Northern Europe	A	34.2	46.6	+36.3
	B	30.3	39.9	+31.7
Southern Europe	A	35.6	55.2	+55.1
	B	31.3	39.1	+24.9
Western Europe	A	36.7	63.8	+73.8
	B	30.2	48.8	+61.6

[1] A: At current labour force participation rates (ILO projections); B: At 1960 labour force participation rates (ILO projections).
Source: ILO: *Economically active population. . .*, op. cit.

ageing of the population would appear far less important, as shown in table 25. In fact, it is unlikely that in future years activity rates could possibly be "rolled back" to 1960 levels. However, this simulation helps to understand the impact on future pension costs of the decline in activity rates which took place in market economy countries between 1960 and 1985.

Let us now return to the influence of unemployment, which, as explained earlier, further reduces the number of people who, through their work, help to finance the cost of pensions.

A further adjustment of the forecasts to take into account the expected rate of unemployment has not been made for all subregions. For certain of them it would be inapplicable (i.e. Eastern Europe, the USSR) and, in any event, the exercise is essentially speculative. A few examples may be enough to support the suggested argument. The countries chosen are the Federal Republic of Germany, the United Kingdom and Yugoslavia. It has been assumed that in these countries the level of unemployment in future years will remain constant at the level recorded in 1985, namely 9.1 per cent in the Federal Republic of Germany, 13.1 per cent in the United Kingdom and 13.3 per cent in Yugoslavia. An alternative forecast assumes that unemployment will decrease in the future until full employment is reached in the year 2025.

The comparison between the alternative forecasts is shown in table 26. If between 1985 and 2025 unemployment could be reduced to zero in

Table 26. Forecast of dependency ratios[1] in 2025 according to alternative unemployment assumptions

| Country | Dependency ratio in 1985 | Dependency ratios in the year 2025 | | | |
| | | Unemployment as in 1985 | | Full employment | |
		Ratio	% increase	Ratio	% increase
Germany, Fed. Rep. of	51.4	87.1	+69.5	70.1	+36.4
United Kingdom	55.2	68.0	+23.2	46.0	−16.7
Yugoslavia	39.8	68.2	+72.6	46.3	+16.3

[1] Ratio of non-employed persons (retired and unemployed) to the economically active population.

the countries selected, the increase in the dependency ratio (a major factor in determining the cost of pensions and related benefits) would be much smaller than if high rates of unemployment were to persist (and, in the United Kingdom, the rate would even decrease).

This example supports the argument that a favourable economic climate and a return to full employment could considerably ease the demographic strain inevitably affecting pension systems in Europe.

A more sophisticated analysis—exceeding the scope of this short chapter—would be required to understand the interdependence between demographic and economic variables in the context of growing pension expenditure. The rate of unemployment is only one economic factor which is difficult to forecast. Mention should be made of the need to take into consideration, for example, future trends in productivity, the health status of the elderly and inflation—all of which are connected, directly or indirectly, to the pension system and its future cost.

The fact remains, none the less, that an ageing population obviously compounds the problem of finding an equitable and affordable approach to the future guarantee of an adequate retirement income for the population as a whole.

FINAL CONSIDERATIONS AND POLICY OPTIONS

The emerging financial imbalance of national pension schemes—causing concern in a number of European countries if one looks towards the end of the century and beyond—can and should be attributed to various factors. One is the unfavourable evolution of the age structure of the population, which is affecting all the countries of Europe to varying degrees.

While some argue that the ageing of the population is the major concern of pension policy, others believe that projected demographic trends—though indeed unfavourable—are not necessarily the major destabilising factor of state pension programmes in the medium and long term. They add that the discussion should focus on the collateral effect on future pension costs of other factors such as: *(a)* the level of benefits and the conditions for entitlement to a pension (including the crucial question of pensionable age); *(b)* the capacity of the country to sustain economic growth and high levels of productive employment; and *(c)* the necessary sharing of responsibility between the State, the individual and the enterprise in provisions for old age (which include an optimum mix between public and private participation), that is, the extent to which a generation can and should save for its own pensions as opposed to relying entirely on inter-generational transfers.

Faced with this multitude of inter-related policy options, and apart from the imperative objective of overcoming their economic difficulties, governments and the social partners have two sets of strategies to consider:

— measures to gradually correct and combat the ageing process itself. These "demographic" means of action are as a rule beyond the competence of social security policy *per se*. Incentives to increase fertility, and measures to improve the financial and environmental conditions for rearing children or stabilise the family, encompass a much wider area of social policy although, as shown in Chapter 2, social security has a definite role to play. The same could be said for measures dealing with international migration as a means of correcting the age distribution of a population.[7] Lengthening of the period of working life (further discussed in Chapter 4) could also be considered under this heading;

— measures applicable to the design and operation of social security pension schemes, and more specifically the review and redirection of those parameters of the pension system which in the long term are bound to put an undue strain on available resources.

To assist in the design of such measures it was thought useful to outline very concisely the range of policy options available to pension planners who have to lay down the foundations for the sound financial development of future pensions.

The options open to policy-makers when planning measures intended to preserve or restore financial balance in public pension schemes affected, inter alia, by unfavourable demographic developments may be directed towards either the sources from which schemes are financed or the range of benefits provided. As a rule, of course, national authorities will endeavour to devise a combination of measures embracing both these strategies, it being clear that a pension system forms a whole and that this makes it very difficult in practice to consider benefits separately from their financial sources.[8]

Measures aimed at sources of financing

With the above reservation in mind, it may be useful to examine here the main spheres of action available to national authorities in their efforts to improve the financial outlook for pension schemes. The comments which follow are of necessity very limited in their scope. The matter is taken up in greater detail in another ILO publication, *Financing social security: The options—An international analysis* (Geneva, 1984), to which the reader is referred. Furthermore, in order to give more tangible substance to the measures listed here, reference—necessarily very brief— will be made to countries which are planning to introduce them or have already introduced them in the recent past. Some of these countries' experiences of social security financing are described earlier in this chapter in more detail (see pp. 86–94).

Intervention by the State with respect to financing mechanisms may take the form of a review of the existing system in order to make readjustments to its internal structure. Thus, the apportionment of social security contributions (whether fixed uniform or wage-related contributions) among the various branches may in some cases be revised, particularly as regards the sharing of the social burden between enterprises and insured persons. In France, for example, contributions levied on wages which, in 1967, represented just over one-third of the overall old-age contribution (3 per cent out of 8.5 per cent) have progressively been increased to 45 per cent of the total in 1987 (6.6 per cent out of 14.8 per cent of the ceiling wages plus 0.1 per cent of total wages under the general schemes). It is true, however, that, for obvious political and social reasons, the scope for readjustment in this field is limited.

At the same time, some thought could be given to the extent to which state budgets, financed by resources which bring into play solidarity mechanisms extending beyond a particular group of wage earners or, more generally speaking, beneficiaries, may be called on to make a more substantial contribution to the financing of social benefits. This technique has already been employed on a number of occasions, mainly in fields where the role of social security goes beyond mere occupational or inter-occupational solidarity. This method, like the preceding one, has its limits, which on the technical side relate mainly to the level and distribution of the existing tax load. It is true that changes might also be envisaged which would result in a lessening of the role of the State, whose share in the financing of old-age benefits would be reduced by increasing recourse to contributions levied on wages or incomes. The Austrian reform referred to earlier aimed to reduce the degree of state involvement (complementary financing to balance the social budget) inasmuch as it both changed the methods of calculating benefits and raised contribution rates by 1 per cent (of which 0.5 per cent was to be paid by the wage earner). Changes in the United Kingdom were also described earlier in this chapter. Table 27 shows percentage changes in the state share of social insurance receipts in various European countries between 1960 and 1983.

In several countries legislation still provides for a ceiling on contributions, whereby wage-related contributions cannot exceed a given maximum, usually calculated annually. It has often been claimed that placing such a ceiling on contributions, which often—though not always—goes hand in hand with a ceiling on benefits, not only limits total social security receipts but may also discourage the use of unskilled labour by increasing its relative cost.[9] Total or partial removal of the ceiling on contributions may also be seen as having—in the short run—a favourable effect on the funds available to pension schemes, since its full impact on the cost of benefits will be felt only after a period which may be longer or shorter depending on the criteria applied in calculating the reference income. Similar reasoning can be applied when the ceiling rises faster than levels of remuneration.

Lastly, inasmuch as certain periods of inactivity (maternity leave, sick leave, unemployment, the rearing of children or occupational risks) may be credited free of charge by pension schemes, it might be worth while to explore the possibility of obtaining compensatory funding, either from the State or from the social security branch which covers the contingency for which the free pension credit is granted. This technique is already being applied—partly at least—in some European countries, including France (old-age insurance for mothers).

Apart from the above-mentioned technical readjustments, whose scope is fairly limited, more substantial changes may be called for in the financing of pension schemes.

Most European schemes operate on a pay-as-you-go basis. As explained earlier in this chapter, this means that the contributions needed to pay current pensions are levied on the income earned by the active population of the moment. It is true that for general schemes it would not seem possible, mainly for technical and financial reasons, to envisage a return to a purely capital funding system (in which current contributions serve to fund all the future liabilities incurred by the working population of that year).

Table 27. State participation in social security receipts, 1960–83 (as a percentage of the total)

Country	1960	1965	1970	1975	1980	1983
Austria	13.7	18.0	20.0	21.6	15.9	20.3
Belgium	25.5	22.7	21.1	28.4	34.1	41.5
Bulgaria	8.0	16.6	34.0	6.1	19.2	n.a.
Czechoslovakia	n.a.	n.a.	96.1	96.2	95.0	94.1
Denmark	52.5	53.9	54.7	82.3	63.9	58.3
Finland	13.6	17.1	15.5	6.8	25.4	26.9
France	6.9	6.6	n.a.	6.3	9.2	10.6
German Dem. Rep.	n.a.	31.3	38.5	47.2	49.7	44.8
Germany, Fed. Rep. of	17.7	22.2	16.8	22.8	19.5	14.6
Greece[1]	n.a.	19.4	21.9	20.7	16.2	21.2
Hungary	37.2	41.7	27.8	n.a.	21.1	n.a.
Ireland	73.0	63.3	59.9	56.9	67.3	65.6
Italy	18.2	22.5	16.7	7.4	32.1	34.5
Luxembourg	16.9	18.7	21.4	19.9	22.0	19.0
Malta	60.6	65.4	61.4	44.7	39.7	38.7
Netherlands	5.9	6.4	8.7	12.4	20.0	12.9
Norway[2]	31.2	25.6	32.3	22.7	37.9	35.9
Portugal[2]	0.8	6.4	n.a.	1.9	6.5	7.8
Romania	32.6	31.4	42.3	32.2	43.6	29.6
Spain	n.a.	n.a.	n.a.	4.3	13.9	20.1
Sweden[2]	54.7	42.9	33.2	34.9	36.7	37.4
Switzerland	9.1	14.7	16.4	14.9	16.1	n.a.
Turkey	n.a.	n.a.	n.a.	n.a.	11.6	5.1
United Kingdom	28.6	22.9	24.9	18.7	46.6	44.3
USSR	n.a.	95.6	95.8	n.a.	96.7	n.a.

[1] Including earmarked taxes. [2] Including participation of local communities.
Source: ILO: *The Cost of Social Security: Twelfth International Inquiry 1981–83*, op. cit.

In particular, any sudden change-over from one financing system to another is judged to be costly and complicated. Nevertheless, certain elements of partial capital funding could, in some cases, be introduced or reintroduced into pension financing without producing too brusque an increase in the social burden: this would at least partly protect pension schemes against the risk of a steep population decline, if not against depreciation in the real value of future benefits. This was the approach adopted in Cyprus, which in 1980 introduced an earnings-related component into its pension scheme: it was calculated that, if legislation remained unchanged, partial funding would in the long run (70 years) lead to equilibrium at lower rates of contribution than those needed to finance a strictly pay-as-you-go system.

However, the reintroduction of capital funding elements into the financing of pension schemes is hardly conceivable in countries in which the burden of financing social security is already a heavy one. Such a change would necessarily require a relatively long-lasting increase in receipts from contributions, inasmuch as the active population would have simultaneously to finance both current pensions and part of the pensions to which they themselves would be entitled in the future.

Still on the subject of modifications likely to influence the final choice of a financing system, attention should be drawn to certain alternative financing arrangements, some of which have already been studied in various countries. These are mainly based on a broadening of the contribution base to include elements other than just wages (or occupational income for the self-employed); inquiries have been made into the expediency, inter alia, of introducing or reintroducing earmarked taxation or of including the value added of the enterprise or the ratio of capital to labour in the manufacturing process when calculating contribution rates. The object of these diverse studies and attempts at reorganisation was mainly to develop the resources from which social security is financed without penalising employment and also, for some risks at least, to dissociate the level of financing from the level of wages, in an attempt to make allowance for the constraints on eligibility imposed by the increased use of part-time labour. The studies are continuing, and the arguments for and against these various options are multiplying without, for the moment at least, any indication as to which of them will prevail.

One possible variant of the preceding solution would be to introduce a sliding scale for contributions on the basis of certain economic and/or social criteria. For instance, it might be feasible to introduce a system whereby labour-intensive enterprises would benefit from lower contribution rates (or lump-sum rebates), the deficit in social receipts to be offset by increased state intervention or by a surtax on capital-intensive enterprises. Several examples of recourse to this method exist in Europe. In Finland, for instance, the rates of employers' contributions to pension schemes take into account the payroll/capital depreciation ratio as a way of favouring labour-intensive enterprises. In Norway employers' contribution rates are lower in areas where it is hoped to increase employment in the interest of regional development. Belgium has introduced a system whereby part of the sums contributed by large firms are redistributed to smaller enterprises.

Here again, the advantages and disadvantages of the method are the subject of much debate, one consideration among others being that it might implicitly encourage disinvestment or discourage modernisation.

However many the factors to be taken into account, the very existence of the technical options briefly listed here shows that, in principle, governments are not defenceless when it comes to dealing with a deteriorating demographic situation—at least as far as their capacity to influence methods of financing pension schemes is concerned.

In addition to measures designed to influence financing, mention should be made here of the possibility of introducing changes in the sharing of responsibilities between the public and private sectors. To be more explicit, such changes would aim to direct compulsory public schemes (and use of the corresponding receipts) more towards the satisfaction of basic needs, by placing the emphasis on the granting of minimum guarantees, while at the same time leaving more freedom of action to complementary schemes, whatever their nature.

Measures aimed at the provision of benefits

Such a change of orientation will obviously have repercussions on the level of social security benefits. Nevertheless, even if they decide not to adopt this particular line of action—or consider it inadvisable—policy-makers still have at their disposal various ways of rationalising benefit provisions: all this does not, of course, take into account the political and social constraints, which in this field often weigh heavily in the balance and to which ample reference has already been made.

Regarding benefits as such, here again decision-makers wishing to exercise firmer control over the growth of pension expenditure have a choice of several areas in which intervention might seem desirable, even though it may not always be feasible in a given national context. The fact is that, whatever the political and social climate of the moment, systems of social protection form part of a society's cultural heritage; in other words, it is hardly possible to contemplate overthrowing the basic philosophy underlying the conditions of eligibility for, and the methods of calculating, benefits. Such action would almost certainly run counter to the social security "model" built up over the years by the national community and would inevitably arouse grave misgivings, to say the least, or even lead to serious rifts in the country's social fabric.[10]

Subject to this reservation—which is an important one—one of the first options available to public authorities seeking to rationalise benefit provisions is to establish a closer relationship between receipts from contributions and the cost of the pensions paid out. In many cases, the current provisions include such methods of calculation that the duration of, and income derived from, contributions have very little influence on the value of the benefits provided. Rights to benefits are created with no guarantee that the funds needed to honour them will be available: obviously, with time, this can lead to serious imbalances in the financing of pension schemes. Among the possible corrective measures are a lengthening of the residence or activity period conferring the right to a full pension, or a lengthening of the contribution period for calculating the reference earnings. One example of this is Spain, where the qualifying period for receipt of a pension has been raised from ten years to 15. In Austria pensions are now based on the earnings of the ten years prior to retirement (instead of five years).[11] Other European countries have already introduced or are thinking of introducing similar measures. Special attention might also be paid to the level and financing of certain specific advantages (credits for having children or for war years, periods considered equivalent to wage-earning periods, etc.), which already exist in a number of pension schemes.

There is, however, no doubt that the most sensitive debate on the subject of the relationship between contributions and pensions centres around the fixing of a *minimum pension*. With a *guaranteed minimum pension*, the link between the level of benefits granted and that of the contributions paid is quite clearly non-existent. However, if this debate is so sensitive, it is obviously because a guaranteed minimum revenue for the aged and/or impoverished members of the population lies at the very heart of the solidarity principles on which social security systems are based; to call into question the merits of this minimum guarantee would, in a way, be to undermine the very foundations on which the institution has been built up. But there is no reason why the conditions of eligibility for a minimum pension within the framework of a contributory scheme should not be a subject for investigation, at least from the point of view of the origin of the resources needed to finance it (occupation-based contributions or state budget). This question has been raised in the past, in France, for instance, where the social security system to some extent relies on the transfer of state funds to finance certain minimum benefits. It is also being widely discussed in Norway, as part of the current debate on the future of that country's pension insurance system (see notes 5 and 8 at the end of this chapter).

Another possibility open to national authorities anxious to preserve or improve the financial equilibrium of their pension schemes is to introduce greater flexibility in the age at which benefits become due or to reconsider the "normal" age for the acquisition of pension rights. It is true that to raise the pensionable age is, politically, a very difficult thing to do, since it would be considered an affront by the social partners, who would see it as an attack on their basic acquired rights. Thus, the Belgian Government's plans some years ago to raise the pensionable age for women to bring it into line with that of men have still not come into effect (see page 89). In Switzerland discussion on the same subject has come up against considerable opposition from trade unions and several political parties. In fact, as can be seen from the examples given on pages 82–83, wherever changes have been made in statutory pensionable age, the tendency has been to lower it rather than to raise it.

The introduction of greater flexibility in the age at which pensions can be drawn would seem to be an easier option, in that it makes more allowance for individual preferences. Mention has already been made of the steps in this direction either already taken or planned in Denmark, Finland, France, Hungary, Norway and Sweden. In France an Act passed in 1987 actually forbids the inclusion in collective agreements of any provisions stipulating a compulsory age for retirement. Such measures may be effective in that they make it possible to postpone the average age at which workers actually retire, on condition of course that they are accompanied by other arrangements (e.g. the adaptation of jobs) which would enable ageing workers to continue in employment. Provisions which allow workers to draw partial pensions while continuing to work on a part-time basis, although not yet very widely accepted, also hold out some promise for the financial future of pension funds by reducing their immediate costs.[12]

A series of other measures can of course be envisaged, as required, by policy-makers seeking ways to rationalise benefit provisions. The formula for calculating pensions can be considered from angles other than just the qualifying period. In addition to the examples already provided, it is worth noting that in Switzerland, where there is no ceiling on contributions, the benefits themselves are calculated within the limits of a maximum reference income. But it is clear that, whatever the national context, it would be extremely difficult to gain acceptance of any sweeping changes in methods of calculating pensions unless they were offset by social gains in some other field: any adjustments, then, must of necessity be limited in their financial scope.

The margin for manoeuvre would seem to be somewhat wider with regard to the adjustment of current pensions, in that measures limiting improvements in pensions strictly to the maintenance of their purchasing power could be looked on as a socially acceptable compromise; the steps in this direction taken in Austria and Belgium have already been referred to. Similarly, restrictions on the simultaneous drawing of wages and pension can often be introduced without too much social upheaval.[13]

In fact, all the measures referred to here are essentially adjustments of existing systems. It is, however, possible to imagine other solutions, of wider scope, aimed at redefining the role or even the very nature of general pension schemes. For example, changes could be made with regard to the respective responsibilities of the State and other parties (local communities, enterprises and occupational groups) and of individuals in the provision of pensions. Here again, the matter is a very sensitive one; it is under discussion in a number of countries, often being referred to by the generic term of "privatisation" or the "withdrawal of the State". This is far too vast a subject to be dealt with in this chapter, though in view of its importance it is worth mentioning.[14] Similarly, there is much debate in many countries on the possibility of sharing the task of income security between social security systems and social assistance mechanisms, the latter being the more flexible in that they do not really generate individual rights; discussion is also under way on the feasibility of making more benefits dependent on the required resources being available within the social security system itself. This debate will no doubt continue to agitate the world of social security over the coming years; its importance is such that it would be worth while devoting specific studies to the subject.[15]

*

* *

However that may be, the list of options described in this section shows how broad is the spectrum of the theoretical solutions open to decision-makers, whether they decide to tackle the problem from the financing angle or from that of the benefits to be provided by the pensions branch. The list may not be exhaustive, but it reflects the broad direction of the studies, proposals for reform and legislative changes now contemplated in Europe.

Naturally each country's specific historical, cultural and social conditions will dictate the set of choices and the margin for manoeuvre allowed by economic constraints. At any event, the commitment to promoting social justice—which is one of the fundamental principles of the International Labour Organisation—suggests that in the process of adapting social security to a changing society, policy-makers should be guided in the pension area by a few basic criteria, such as:

— a fair and equitable distribution between all citizens, at any given time, of the financial support required by pension policies;

— the allocation of resources in a way that ensures the protection of those categories of the population with the greatest needs;

— the spreading, as equitably as possible, of the cost of pensions between successive generations;

— consideration of the social protection of the elderly not in isolation but within the broad framework of all social security needs of the population.

Notes

[1] See, in particular, G. Tamburi and P. Mouton: "The uncertain frontier between private and public pension schemes", in International Social Security Association (ISSA): *Conjugating public and private: The case of pensions,* Studies and Research No. 24 (Geneva, 1987), pp. 29–43.

[2] See, in particular, M. Tracy: *Retirement age practices in ten industrial societies, 1960–1976,* Studies and Research No. 14 (Geneva, ISSA, 1979).

[3] Relevant studies recently published by the ILO addressing pension problems include: *Pensions and inflation* (Geneva, 1977); *Financing social security: The options* (Geneva, 1984); *Into the twenty-first century: The development of social security* (Geneva, 1984); J. J. Carroll: *Early retirement practices in selected European countries* (Geneva, 1985; mimeographed; out of print); G. Tamburi: *Commitments of national pension systems in OECD countries: Strategies for dealing with the future,* ILO Contribution to a Joint Japanese/OECD Conference on Health and Pensions Policies in the Context of Demographic Evolution and Economic Constraints, Tokyo, 1985 (mimeographed).

[4] Commissariat général du Plan; *Vieillir solidaires* (Paris, La Documentation française, 1986).

[5] A. Hatland: *The future of Norwegian social insurance* (Oslo, Institute of Applied Social Research, 1986).

[6] OECD: *Social expenditure 1960–1990* (Paris, 1985).

[7] A study was recently conducted in Luxembourg (*Quelques réflexions sur le défi démographique et la sécurité sociale au Luxembourg,* 1987), a country where resident migrant workers accounted for 30 per cent of the internal active population in 1981—account not being taken of border workers representing a further 11 per cent of the active population. The study concluded that, in the Luxembourg context, "the debate on the demographic impact leads back, in fact, to an economic challenge, this apart from the thorny question of integration".

[8] The Norwegian study (see note 5, above) is significant in this respect. The author of the report submits ten questions for study by the authorities, most of them directly concerned both with financing and with the nature of benefits. It is clear, for instance, that the proposals concerning retirement age and its flexibility, and the introduction of partial pensions, are not neutral, either from the point of view of benefits or from that of financing. Similarly, changes in the rules concerning complementary pension schemes, the drawing of pensions while continuing to work, equal treatment for men and women and the tax regulations for retired persons, and so on, affect both the level of benefits and their attractiveness, as well as the total resources devoted to maintaining old people's incomes. As a corollary, any substantial broadening of the pension-financing base, for example, by increasing the share of state financing, would generally bring about a parallel change in the basic philosophy of the system, which would move more towards the provision of subsistence allowances based on such criteria as needs and income levels.

[9] This was the view taken by the independent group of experts invited by the Director-General of the ILO to inquire into the future of social security in industrial countries (*Into the twenty-first century: The development of social security* (Geneva, 1984), para. 189).

[10] See, in particular, Tamburi, op. cit., para. 12.

[11] See pp. 90–91 and 89 of this chapter for Spain and Austria respectively.

[12] As early as 1976, T. G. Staples drew attention to the possibility of an integrated definition of eligibility for pensions in which age would be only one one factor among many, such as working conditions, state of health or loss of earnings. See "Trends in the definition of risk in old age and invalidity schemes", in *International Social Security Review* (Geneva, ISSA), No. 2, 1978, pp. 173–186.

[13] A "solidarity contribution" penalising the simultaneous drawing of wages and pension was introduced in France in 1983, at the same time as the normal pensionable age was reduced, on certain conditions, from 65 to 60 years. This provision was annulled in 1986.

[14] See, inter alia, ISSA: *Conjugating public and private: The case of pensions,* op. cit.

¹⁵ The debate on the "guaranteed social minimum" obviously forms part of this theme. In Western Europe five countries had introduced an all-in payment of this nature before 1988: the Federal Republic of Germany (1962), the United Kingdom (1966), Belgium (1974), Denmark (after 1933) and the Netherlands (where the minimum guaranteed income for a couple without children is equal to the minimum wage and for a single person 70 per cent of that amount). In France a draft Bill brought in by the Government in May 1988 aims to extend to the whole country the minimum wage introduced several years ago on an experimental basis in a number of municipalities.

THE AGEING OF THE POPULATION IN EUROPE AND THE COST OF HEALTH CARE

4

The predicted ageing of the population in Europe will have repercussions on all aspects of family, social and economic life. This chapter is devoted to the problems this ageing will raise with regard to health: it examines the ways in which health care systems may be adjusted and medical expenditure financed.

After a brief description of the general characteristics of schemes for the collective coverage of health expenditure in Europe, it will attempt to assess the impact of increased numbers of older people on the demand for medical care. This assessment will be based on the data available as regards both the expected demographic developments in Europe over the next 30 years and the level and structure of medical expenditure in relation to age. It should be pointed out here that the scarcity of data on the subject has made it impossible to provide more than just a few numerical examples; these do, however, indicate the broad trends in most, if not all, European countries.

This first part will be followed by a discussion of past and possible future policies for the provision of care designed to meet the specific needs of older people, and for the financing of such care. Examples from various European countries will be given, although the study does not claim to provide an exhaustive catalogue of all the measures taken over the past few years.

COLLECTIVE COVERAGE OF MEDICAL EXPENDITURE THROUGH SOCIAL SECURITY SYSTEMS AND THE PROVISION MADE FOR THE ELDERLY

Although this chapter of our study on the inter-relations between demographic development and social security in no way sets out to analyse all the methods by which European countries provide collective coverage of health care expenditure or access to medical care, it may be useful to start with a very general survey of the main provisions adopted by them. In addition, in order to facilitate understanding of the specific problems faced by older people, some explanations with regard to these provisions—again very general—will be given concerning their position, and that of retired persons in particular.

It may be assumed that social (or collective) coverage of health care expenditure is provided by one of the following forms of organisation[1]— optional health care schemes, compulsory health insurance, national health insurance or national health services.

An optional health scheme implies that it is up to the individual to decide whether or not to belong to an insurance institution guaranteeing the coverage of his or her health expenditure. This type of scheme is very rare in Europe, at least as a form of basic or main coverage. It is nevertheless the rule in Switzerland, where the relevant federal legislation has not instituted compulsory health insurance. Therefore, in most of the territorial subdivisions (cantons), citizens are not required to take out insurance; however, in accordance with federal legislation, some cantons have made health insurance compulsory, but generally only for those in the lowest income groups. Although most of the residents are in fact covered by health insurance, this is mainly because they themselves have decided to take this step.

Apart from the fact that such insurance is individual rather than family based, funds are able to impose a form of selection on the risks they insure; they may, for example, turn down applications for membership made by persons over a certain age and express "reservations" about providing coverage for illnesses existing before membership.

Compulsory health insurance makes entitlement to medical care (or the reimbursement of expenses incurred) subject to the payment of contributions by the insured persons and, if need be, by the employers. Although this type of system has been losing ground over the years, geographically at least, and giving way to more universal schemes, it is nevertheless still in force in many countries such as Austria, the Benelux countries, France, the Federal Republic of Germany and Yugoslavia.

National health insurance differs from compulsory health insurance mainly in that, apart from its universal nature, it does not make entitlement to benefit subject to the payment of contributions, even when the system of compulsory contributions exists. This kind of scheme may be financed in various ways, for example, by state subsidies, by income-related as opposed to merely wage-related contributions by the insured person, and by the standard employers' and/or wage earner's contributions. It is found in Finland (out-patient care), the Netherlands (long-term care), Norway and Sweden (covering the whole of the resident population).

Although *national health services* are also universal schemes and, in principle, cover the full range of preventive and curative care, they differ from the systems mentioned above in that it is one and the same body which finances and dispenses care, in this instance the public authority. Apart from this common feature, national health services may vary considerably depending upon the country, and may or may not co-exist with private health care systems or with one or several different health insurance schemes. At present, national health services are very widespread in Europe and may be found in all the subregions of the continent, including the United Kingdom (which was the forerunner in Western Europe), Greece, Iceland, Italy, Portugal and almost all the Eastern European countries.

Following this short description of the organisational arrangements for collective coverage of health expenditure in Europe, any study of the links between demographic development and medical care must necessarily include a brief survey of the specific situation of older persons under these schemes—retired persons in particular.

It is hardly surprising that insurance schemes based on a national health service or on national health insurance treat pensioners, very generally speaking, in the same way as all other residents. There may, however, be some slight differences, as for instance in Ireland, where the ceiling on incomes, beyond which a person is no longer entitled to what is called "full" coverage, is higher for pensioners than for those gainfully employed, and in the United Kingdom, where deductions are made from the pension in the case of long-term hospitalisation. In the Eastern European countries pensioners, or some categories among them, sometimes come under slightly different rules from those applying to the gainfully employed.

Under compulsory health insurance schemes, specific regulations may be applied to pensioners, especially with respect to financing. For instance, health insurance contributions are deducted from pensions in Belgium (provided that the pension does not then fall below a prescribed minimum), France, the Federal Republic of Germany[2] (where a scheme was introduced in 1983, and rates increased by stages up to 1985) and Luxembourg (where the contributions are shared between the pensioner and the pension fund). In Yugoslavia the financing of pensioners' health care is met totally by the institution providing the benefit, in the form of a contribution paid to the local health insurance association.

Finally, as regards optional health schemes, mention has already been made of the restrictive measures which may be applied by health insurance funds on grounds of age or pre-existing illnesses.

Furthermore, in many cases, older persons or pensioners are entitled to more favourable benefits than other insured categories, under conditions which will be briefly described later in this chapter.

DEMOGRAPHY, HEALTH AND MEDICAL EXPENDITURE

Given the slowing down of economic growth experienced lately by most European countries, the predicted increase in the number of older persons is giving rise to growing fears about how social protection in general—and health care coverage in particular—is to be financed. In order to measure the extent of the problem, at least approximately, the study must take into account the population projections for the coming years and current knowledge concerning the changes in health and health care needs that accompany advancing age. The data given in Chapter 1 will serve as the basis for the calculations. There is no need to remind the reader here of the obvious trend towards the ageing of Europe's population; this is made quite clear throughout the study.

The health of older persons

The statistical findings of studies carried out in various countries on the relationship between demographic variables and a population's state of health have led their authors to a number of conclusions which do not, however, always coincide. Nevertheless, there is general agreement on the following points:

1. The health of older persons cannot be described as that of a homogeneous group; whatever the lower age limit assigned to the group, it will always contain some individuals who are younger and some who are older; their state of health and their requirements in the way of medical care may vary widely according to sex, family background, and social and economic milieu.

2. The morbidity of older persons is characterised by a multitude of pathological states: a survey from the United Kingdom[3] reports an average of 3.5 serious conditions for old people living outside hospitals and six for those in hospital.

3. The average number of illnesses per person increases with age: in 1980 in France, persons questioned declared the existence of 1.7 illnesses between 2 and 15 years of age, 2.4 between 16 and 39, 4.3 between 40 and 60, 6.2 between 65 and 79, and 6.4 after the age of 80.[4]

4. The morbidity of older persons is composed both of major chronic conditions[5]—cardiovascular disease, cancer, diabetes, high blood pres-

sure, osteo-articular disease, respiratory diseases—and by less serious complaints, such as sight and hearing disorders, which nevertheless disrupt everyday life. Among the psychiatric illnesses affecting the elderly, the most frequent is Alzheimer's disease (senile dementia), for which there is at present no known treatment and which, therefore, attracts particularly close attention. It has been calculated that dementia may affect as many as 6.3 per cent of those in the over-65 age group, the rate rising from 2.1 per cent between the ages of 65 and 69 to 17.7 per cent after the age of 80.[6]

5. It is mainly very old people, especially those over 75 or 80 years of age, who suffer the really serious problems of disablement or dependency.[7] An inquiry carried out in Gothenburg (Sweden) among 70 year-olds revealed that most of them were in good physical and mental shape, that only 3 per cent needed to be in an institution and that 18 per cent needed help in their own homes. In the Netherlands in 1984, 83 per cent of men and 80 per cent of women between the ages of 65 and 69 reported no limitation of their activities, these proportions falling to 62 per cent and 47 per cent respectively for those over 80 years of age.

6. It is after the age of 75 or 80 that home treatment becomes more difficult and institutional care becomes more frequent. In the Netherlands in 1980, the percentage of old persons in institutions was 8.1 for the over-65s in general, ranging from 0.6 per cent between the ages of 65 and 69 and 41.2 per cent after the age of 90;[8] at all ages the rates were higher for women than for men. In France 9.1 per cent of people over the age of 75 were living in institutions whereas, for all those aged 60 and over, the proportion was only half as great (4.7 per cent).[9] In Sweden 1 per cent of all 65–69 year-olds were cared for in institutions, the percentage rising to 31 per cent for the over-80s.[10] In the German Democratic Republic the number of places provided in long-term care establishments was, in 1983, 4.5 per cent of the total number of persons in the corresponding age groups. It is estimated that in Czechoslovakia 6 per cent of retired people need more or less permanent social or medical assistance and that 3 per cent should, for health reasons, be in institutions providing long-term care. In 1984 Hungary reported 2 per cent of persons over the age of 60 as living in institutions, the percentage being twice as high for men as for women. Of the total number, however, the rates for those over the age of 70 were 49 per cent for men and 72 per cent for women: this would seem to indicate that women enter such establishments later in life than men.[11]

7. Although the life expectancy of women is about eight years higher at birth than that of men, and a little over three years higher at the age of 60, women claim to have more illnesses than men; indeed, there is a higher level of disability among women than among men.[12]

8. In general, the elderly tend to underestimate the seriousness of their illnesses and to look on any discomfort as "normal". A survey carried out by the World Health Organization (WHO) in 15 districts or regions of Europe[13] has revealed wide variations between the numbers declaring themselves as not being in good health. Among men from 65 to 69 years of age, for instance, the proportion making this assertion was 41 per cent in Brussels, but only 19 per cent in nearby Leuven. The highest proportions (more than 70 per cent considering themselves not to be in good health) were found in Tampere (Finland), Bialystok (Poland) and Kiev (USSR). It should also be noted that the percentage of persons "not feeing well" sometimes declines with age, a seeming paradox which may bear out the hypothesis that very old people underestimate the gravity of their illnesses (see table 28).

9. During the past few years, life expectancy at birth has made great advances in Europe, as can be seen from figures 2 and 3. It has increased from 65.3 years (1950–55) to 72.2 years (1980–85), reflecting the drop in mortality rates for almost all age groups. Between 1970 and the early 1980s, life expectancy at 65 years of age also rose, with an increase of 1.1 years for women and 0.6 years for men (figures 2*(a)* and *(b)*). In the case of older people, the drop in overall mortality was mainly apparent after 1970, being linked to a fall in mortality rates from cardiovascular disease. The case of the USSR is also worth noting; following the introduction in 1985 of certain measures designed to promote healthier life-styles, the overall mortality rates from 1986 onwards declined from 10.6 to 9.7 per cent.

But can life expectancy be used as an indicator of a population's state of health and of improvements in this health? At present, there are differing views on the subject. Some believe that the extension of life expectancy and improvements in health have gone hand in hand and that the state of health of a 70 year-old today is much better than that of a 60 year-old 25 years ago.[14] This bears out the finding that, in the Parisian region of France, the proportion of old persons unable to lead a normal life has fallen from 50 per cent to 29 per cent in 15 years, as a result of a decline in the numbers suffering from serious disabilities—and this despite an increase in the number of minor handicaps.[15]

There are those who reject this optimistic point of view, claiming that the progress achieved with regard to mortality rates, by keeping diseases in check rather than curing them, has not brought about a corresponding increase in *active* life expectancy but has led to a high level of chronic morbidity and handicaps amongst the survivors. This theory is, however, to some extent invalidated by the effect of maintaining older people in their jobs—with suitable adaptation of their working conditions—as is done in most of the Eastern European countries.

Table 28. Percentages of elderly people not feeling healthy (in representative samples)

Area/district	Age group (years)											
	Men						Women					
	60–64	65–69	70–74	75–79	80–84	85–89	60–64	65–69	70–74	75–79	80–84	85–89
Brussels (Belgium)	55	41	33	65	63	20	59	54	48	55	60	45
Leuven (Belgium)	21	19	22	23	19	16	26	19	35	21	17	17
Berlin (West)[1]	47	44	46	55	56	57	48	50	64	66	67	66
Tampere (Finland)	70	79	68	59	70	65	66	76	65	71	77	61
Midi-Pyrénées (France)	31	27	29	33	27	29	30	36	36	39	41	37
Upper Normandy (France)	17	33	25	29	43	14	29	40	41	44	41	57
Rural Greece	42	46	56	64	69	83	55	68	81	73	76	81
Florence (Italy)	13	24	31	18	17	20	37	38	32	34	39	36
Low Ombrone (Italy)	41	29	33	41	33	47	56	49	54	51	59	51
West Amiata (Italy)	28	33	24	33	34	31	39	28	44	47	32	28
Bialystok (Poland)	55	72	77	77	86	—	69	73	78	81	89	—
Bucharest (Romania)	67	65	74	90	81	89	86	86	91	88	89	90
Kiev (USSR)	72	75	82	81	79	88	83	84	90	89	91	94
Belgrade (Yugoslavia)	35	42	42	52	45	52	45	50	57	57	62	59
Zagreb (Yugoslavia)	65	55	74	69	76	67	66	73	72	76	85	78

[1] The interests of Berlin (West) are represented in the International Labour Office by the Federal Republic of Germany.

Source: WHO, Regional Office for Europe: *The elderly in eleven countries: A socio-medical survey*, Public Health in Europe, 21 (Copenhagen, 1983), table 18.

From pyramid to pillar

Figure 2(a): Changes in life expectancy for women between 1970 and 1979–83[1]

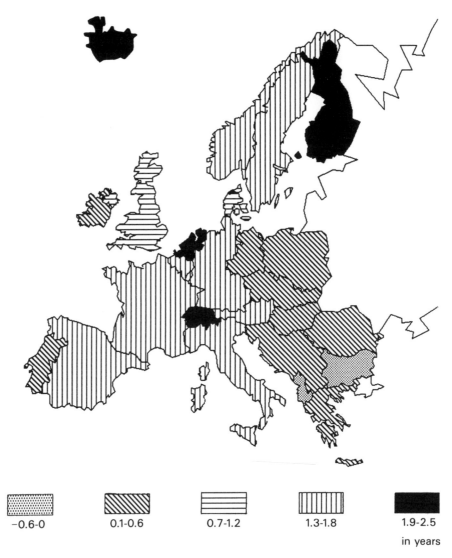

−0.6-0	0.1-0.6	0.7-1.2	1.3-1.8	1.9-2.5

in years

[1] Years vary from country to country.
Source: Data provided by the WHO Regional Office for Europe.

124

Figure 2(*b*): Changes in life expectancy for men between 1970 and 1979–83[1]

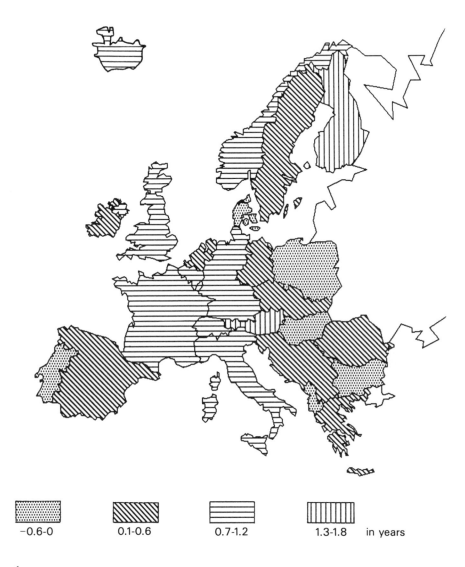

| −0.6-0 | 0.1-0.6 | 0.7-1.2 | 1.3-1.8 | in years |

[1] Years vary from country to country.
Source: Data provided by the WHO Regional Office for Europe.

From pyramid to pillar

Figure 3(a): Life expectancy at age 65 for women, 1979–83[1]

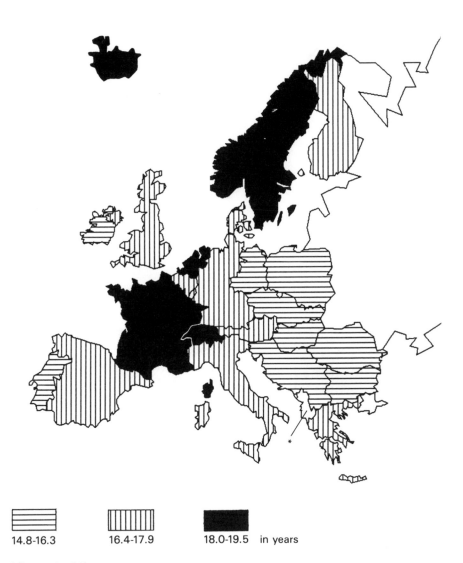

| 14.8-16.3 | 16.4-17.9 | 18.0-19.5 | in years |

* Figures not available

[1] Years vary from country to country.

Source: Data provided by the WHO Regional Office for Europe.

Figure 3(*b*): Life expectancy at age 65 for men, 1979–83¹

11.6-13.1	13.2-14.7	14.8-16.3	in years

* Figures not available
¹ Years vary from country to country.
Source: Data provided by the WHO Regional Office for Europe.

On the subject of older persons' state of health, there are other questions which are much debated:

— Does the decline of health with age reflect an inevitable ageing process or does it result from the building up and interaction of illnesses which might have been treated or prevented? If the latter is the case, early diagnosis of pathological conditions at all ages and their early treatment could limit the ill-effects and help to improve the health of the elderly.

— Has medical care contributed significantly towards lengthening life expectancy or do the improvements recorded rather reflect enhanced life-styles and better economic conditions?

— Can it be envisaged that life expectancy will continue to rise in the coming years or will it level off? Similarly, will there be improvements in health, especially that of very old people?

It is to be hoped that analyses of population groups over time will enable researchers to find clear answers to these questions. Such issues are crucial in projecting the health needs of ageing populations and establishing policies that will enable these needs to be met, either by improving the access of older persons to medical care as a whole or by giving priority attention to organising facilities in the institutions that will look after them.

Medical expenditure according to age and sex

In many countries statistics drawn from surveys or administrative sources show quite clearly that the level and structure of medical expenditure vary considerably according to the demographic factors of age and sex. Depending on the nature of the information provided by these sources, analysis may be more or less elaborate. All the studies show that expenditure is highest for very young children and older persons, with a rapid increase after 45 years of age; some of them use more detailed age groups and categories and are therefore more refined in their results.

To describe the links between demographic variables and health care consumption, reference will be made at this point to data concerning the Netherlands and France, which illustrate three aspects particularly well: variations in levels of health care consumption according to age and sex; their differential development over time; and the contribution of various demographic groups to medical expenditure. It may be assumed that the studies carried out for these two countries have a wider scope, and their results are set out in table 29.

The main findings are as follows:

— in both countries, older people have far greater recourse to medical care than younger people and this gap widens with age. This is particularly the case in the Netherlands, where the effect of long-term care in nursing homes is more fully covered in the statistics;

— women have a completely different age-related medical profile from men, due naturally to the influence of child bearing on the health-care consumption of the 15–44 age group;

Table 29. Variations in medical expenditure by age and sex, France, 1980, and the Netherlands, 1982 (index of medical expenditure per head: 100 = 15–44 age group)

Age group	Overall health care			
	Men		Women	
	France	Netherlands	France	Netherlands
Under 15 years	105.4	108.8	61.7	71.6
15 to 44 years	100.0	100.0	100.0	100.0
45 to 64 years	221.7	172.3	133.3	126.7
65 to 74 years	366.9	318.2	198.3	221.2
75 years and over	395.3	648.9	206.3	508.7
All ages	156.7	148.7	121.1	133.4

Age group	Out-patient care			
	Men		Women	
	France	Netherlands	France	Netherlands
Under 15 years	112.6	100.9	64.1	62.1
15 to 44 years	100.0	100.0	100.0	100.0
45 to 64 years	206.8	143.6	144.0	99.6
65 to 74 years	361.0	172.3	191.2	140.5
75 years and over	330.8	248.8	223.3	223.8
All ages	152.2	118.5	124.7	102.7

Table 29. (cont.)

Age group	Institutional care			
	Men		Women	
	France[1]	Netherlands[2]	France[1]	Netherlands[2]
Under 15 years	97.3	116.7	59.5	81.8
15 to 44 years	100.0	100.0	100.0	100.0
45 to 64 years	238.2	198.0	122.8	154.8
65 to 74 years	373.5	447.3	205.4	305.4
75 years and over	466.8	1 005.7	189.4	804.4
All ages	161.8	175.8	117.5	165.4

[1] Covers mainly short- and medium-term hospital care.   [2] Covers care provided in hospitals and nursing homes.
Sources: France: INSEE-CREDES Inquiries 1970 and 1980. Findings analysed and published mainly by the National Institute of Statistics and Economic Studies (INSEE) and the Centre for Research, Studies and Documentation on Health Expenditure (CREDES) (formally Medical Finances Division of CREDOC); Netherlands: Central Bureau of Statistics.

— variations in age-related medical expenditure are more or less pronounced according to the type of care dispensed, with growth rates seemingly more rapid and earlier for institutional care (hospitals and nursing homes);

— as regards out-patient care, French experience has shown that the widest divergence between age groups would seem to occur in the consumption of pharmaceuticals.

Figures 4 to 8 illustrate these points quite clearly.

It should be recalled, furthermore, that a survey also carried out in France from 1970 to 1980[16] revealed that health expenditure over a period of time increased more rapidly for old people and young children than for the population as a whole; in other words, the higher the initial consumption of a specific age group, the more pronounced will be its relative increase over time. This finding should, of course, wherever it is borne out by the facts, be taken into account when making projections for the consumption of health care by what is expected to be an ageing population.

Although the results of the surveys carried out in France and the Netherlands cannot, naturally, be directly applied to other countries,

Figure 4: Variations in medical expenditure by age and sex, the Netherlands, 1982 (per head, in guilders)

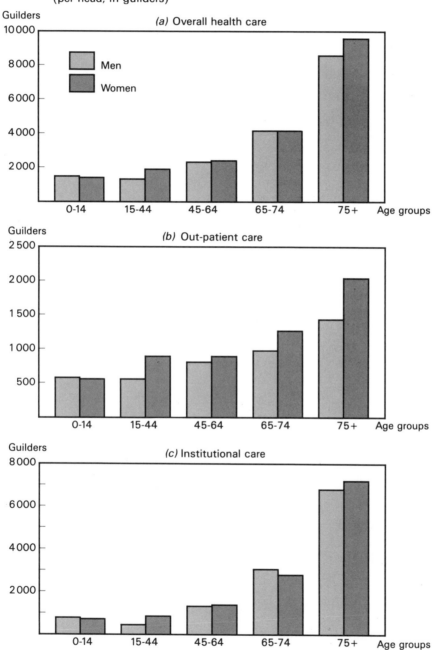

Source: The Netherlands, Central Bureau of Statistics.

Figure 5: Hospital admissions by age and sex, the Netherlands, 1983 (number per 100 persons)

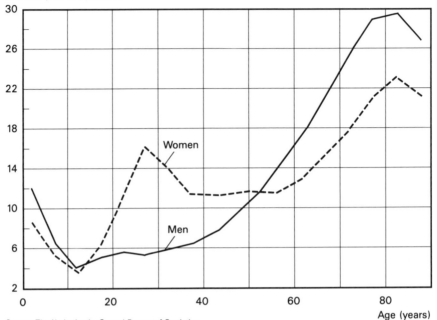

Source: The Netherlands, Central Bureau of Statistics.

they nevertheless provide an interesting basis upon which to build future projections. It might be relevant to point out here that these data are partially borne out by the findings of less comprehensive surveys conducted in other countries.

Thus, in the United Kingdom, average expenditure on persons aged 65–74 was, in 1981–82, 1.8 times the average for the population as a whole. In the Federal Republic of Germany this average was 2.5 times as high for the over-75s, and 7.8 times when hospital care was provided. In Finland, in the early 1980s, the average number of days spent in hospital annually was 2.3 for the under-65s, 12.4 for persons between the ages of 65 and 74, 29.5 for those aged between 75 and 84, and 91 for those aged over 85.[17]

When thus comparing the level of medical consumption of different age groups and attempting to project the findings of this comparison into

Figure 6: Visits to general practitioners by age and sex, the Netherlands, 1983/84 (number per person)

Number per person

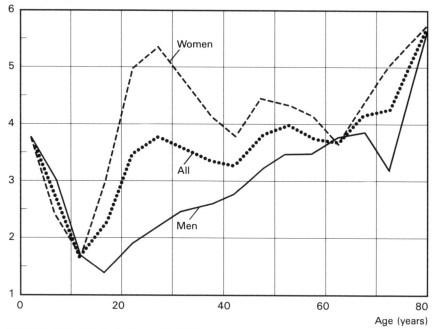

Source: The Netherlands, Central Bureau of Statistics.

the fairly distant future, it must be borne in mind that the "generation effect" probably influences to a great extent both the attitude of sick elderly persons and their families towards medical care and the behaviour of those caring for them. An older person's state of health is obviously linked to various social and environmental aspects of the life led by the individual up to that point and to his or her current social and economic integration, as well as to former illnesses and the way they were treated.

Similarly, the way in which the older person views his or her symptoms and decides to have them treated depends both upon adjustment to present-day economic and technological conditions and upon attitudes that date from a very different period. The question therefore arises whether the medical consumption of old and very old persons, although relatively high, always meets their needs.

Figure 7: Medical expenditure by age, France, 1980[1] (per head, in francs)

Per head in francs

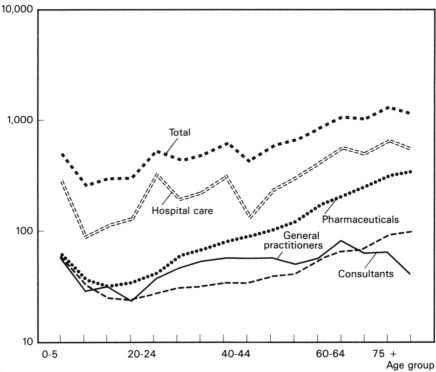

There is probably less incertitude on this point in countries which, like a number of Eastern European countries, dispense medical care within the general framework of a national health system but by districts or subregions sufficiently small to permit individual home-based follow-up care of old people by skilled personnel.

Some examples are Czechoslovakia, the German Democratic Republic, Romania and the USSR. In Czechoslovakia, for instance, when the percentage of old people in a particular district is high, a district geriatric specialist is appointed and assisted by expert paramedical staff.

Figure 8: Index of medical expenditure by age, France, 1970 and 1980 (index: 100 = age group 5–9 years)

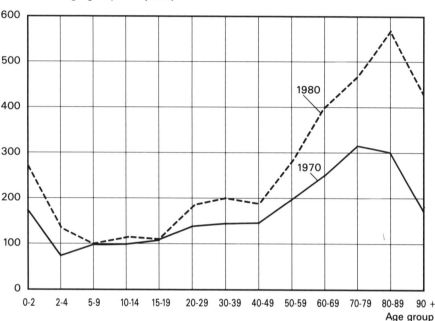

Source: INSEE-CREDOC Inquiries, 1970 and 1980. Results analysed and published mainly by INSEE and CREDES (formerly Medical Finances Division of CREDOC).

Does the ageing of the population necessarily entail a sharper increase in medical expenditure?

The ageing of the population is often held up as a factor which will cause even greater imbalances in health care budgets, because it is believed that it will contribute to the increase in medical expenditure and the corresponding benefits, without being offset by increased resources— all this in a climate in which the financing of collective social protection agencies may run into difficulties, mainly because of the slowing down of economic growth. Systems which are not financed from contributions are, of course, also subject to constraints which can, broadly speaking, be linked to the growth rate of national income and the ways in which it is put to use.

This theory is so bound up with the view—based on observation—that medical consumption is higher among older people that decision-makers, when considering how to cope with this problem, fail to look into the quantitative dimension of the trend. However, existing data, of which a brief summary appears earlier in this chapter, enable us to evaluate the direct effect that the ageing of the population has on health expenditure according to different hypotheses.

Two of these hypotheses are considered here: the first is that the relative variations in average medical consumption between the various age groups, as can be observed at present, will be maintained in the future; the second, in line with the analysis of past trends, is based on an accentuation of these variations.

According to the *first hypothesis*, medical consumption per head would increase at the same rate for all age groups. On the basis of the United Nations medium variant for the population of Europe in 2000 and 2015, combined with data on medical consumption by detailed age group for France in 1980 and the Netherlands in 1982, it was possible to calculate the increase in medical expenditure over the next 30 years resulting solely from distortion of the age pyramid in different countries. The conclusion was that the influence of the "ageing factor" alone on the increase in medical expenditure would be extremely slight (table 30) compared with past growth rates in the countries in question.

The data for France and the Netherlands, which do not cover completely identical fields, give slightly different results which are, nevertheless, largely of the same order of magnitude. In the most extreme case, it is estimated that average medical expenditure per person in Europe will increase by 9.3 per cent between 1985 and 2015, i.e. by an average of 0.3 per cent per year, for health care as a whole. Annual increases will represent a maximum of 0.4 per cent for institutional care (Netherlands data which include care in nursing homes) and 0.2 per cent in the out-patient sector (French data).

Surprisingly, these rates seem relatively low compared with the increases noted all over Europe and in other parts of the world in recent years. They are, however, similar to those forecast earlier in France, the Federal Republic of Germany, Sweden, the United Kingdom, and the United States.[18]

In fact, the reason that the ageing of the population has only a slight effect on medical expenditure, in spite of the rapid increase in the number of people seeking medical care as they get older, is that changes in the age structure of a population are a relatively slow process. A study prepared by the International Monetary Fund (IMF)[19] points out that, if the ageing of the population were the only factor in the increase of medical expenditure, the share of expenditure in GDP would rapidly decline.

Table 30. Increase in medical expenditure in Europe on the basis of two sources of age-related variations in medical consumption (index: 1985 = 100)

Type of expenditure	Men		Women		Both sexes	
	A[1]	B[2]	A[1]	B[2]	A[1]	B[2]
Out-patient care						
2000	102.0	104.5	101.9	102.6	101.9	103.3
2015	104.9	109.6	103.8	105.6	104.2	107.2
Institutional care						
2000	105.5	104.8	105.2	101.5	105.3	102.8
2015	113.7	108.7	111.5	102.1	112.4	104.8
Total care						
2000	104.2	104.6	103.9	102.1	104.0	103.1
2015	110.5	109.2	108.5	104.0	109.3	106.1

[1] Source A: Netherlands data; care in nursing homes (and specialised long-term establishments) is included.
[2] Source B: French data; care in long-term establishments is underestimated.
Sources: Netherlands: Central Bureau of Statistics, 1982; France: INSEE-CREDES Inquiry, 1980.

However, the hypothesis of homogeneous growth is only an initial approach which contradicts studies of earlier periods. In the past the demand for medical treatment, linked to changes in the supply system—staff, equipment and technology—and in social welfare, was, on the whole, characterised by a more rapid increase in medical consumption in groups which already had a high consumption, in particular among older people, as can be seen from table 31.

A *second hypothesis* therefore consists in carrying such a trend forward, calculating the growth rates for the various age groups on the same basis as those contained in the French data for the 1970–80 period. It is thus estimated that there will be an increase in medical expenditure, brought about solely by the ageing of the population in Europe, of 25 per cent between 1985 and 2015 (table 32). The corresponding average *annual* increase will in this case be 0.8 per cent, which is still much lower than the increases in medical expenditure incurred in the past few years, but 0.5 per cent higher than the figure reached by adopting the hypothesis of homogeneous growth by age group (0.3 per cent). This result may, however, be low in comparison with the most likely developments, in that

Table 31. Increase in medical expenditure per head, by age group, France, 1970–80

Age group (years)	Increase, 1970–80 Average annual increase at constant prices (%)
Under 5	8.9
5–9	3.3
10–14	4.6
15–19	4.0
20–29	6.1
30–39	6.7
40–49	5.8
50–59	7.0
60–69	8.5
70–79	7.4
80 and over	10.1
All ages	6.9

Source: INSEE-CREDES Inquiries, 1970 and 1980.

Table 32. Level of medical consumption per head according to several assumptions[1] and population structures in Europe (index: 1985 = 100)

Extrapolated medical consumption per head[1]	Population structure in Europe in		
	1985	2000	2015
1985 level	100.00	103.38	107.13
2000 level	102.45	107.14	113.11
2015 level	110.36	116.60	125.47

[1] The 1985, 2000 and 2015 levels of medical consumption are calculated on the basis of the 1980 French data, assuming that the differential growth rates for the various age groups remain the same as those of 1970–80.

the cost of long-term institutional care was underestimated in the basic French data.

Whatever the case, in the long-term projections envisaged here, there are too many uncertainties as to the development of behavioural patterns to be able to determine which hypothesis is the more realistic. First, there is no way of knowing how the health care needs of the various population groups who have not experienced the same life-styles or been exposed to the same health education or preventive measures will develop; second, it cannot be foreseen to what extent the medical consumption of different age groups will be influenced by future technological developments which might change both the way certain illnesses are treated and the cost of this treatment, and by the policies of collective financing bodies.

The policy measures practised by many governments to bring medical expenditure under control might affect various groups of the population to varying degrees and, consequently, the different age groups. This can be illustrated by the following examples:

— if the growth of medical expenditure slows down at the same rate as hitherto for all age groups, the growth will nevertheless remain faster for older than for young people; this, in conjunction with the ageing of the population, will itself result in a slight speeding up of the growth in expenditure as a whole.[20] This is in line with the second hypothesis outlined above. If a fairly low level of increase in medical consumption were aimed at for the population as a whole, the result might be a drop in medical consumption for certain age groups, especially young adults;[21]

— it is only by introducing a policy designed to reduce the increase in the medical expenditure of older persons to a greater extent than that of younger persons that the hypothesis of uniform growth could be confirmed in the future. The French example shows that, in order to obtain parallel rates of increase for the over-65 and the 5–20 year-old age groups, the growth rate of medical costs would have to be reduced by 4 percentage points more for the first group than for the second. In other words, a uniform average annual growth in medical expenditure of 3 per cent would imply a reduction of 1 percentage point in the growth rate for the younger groups (from 4 to 3 per cent) and a reduction of 5 percentage points for old persons, whose growth rate would have to fall from 8 per cent to 3 per cent.

However, in most countries measures to reduce the medical consumption of younger people or a much stricter policy towards older people than towards other categories of the population could not be implemented without running into opposition from those concerned. Furthermore, it goes without saying that any such action would be incompatible with the principles and policies increasingly pursued in many European countries, where the clearly defined goal is to ensure the best possible levels of health for all, both quantitively and qualitatively. Subtler policies are more likely to be chosen and it is, therefore, reasonable to estimate that the rate of increase in medical consumption brought about solely by the ageing of the population in Europe will be about 0.5 per cent per year between 1985 and 2015, representing a value half-way between the estimates reached by using the above two hypotheses—which may be regarded as extremes. The results of simulations by country for the two hypotheses are given in the statistical appendix, tables A.7. and A.8.

POLICIES TO PROVIDE HEALTH CARE FOR THE ELDERLY

The second part of this chapter has shown that although the ageing of the population undoubtedly contributes to increasing medical expenditure, its real impact, which is relatively modest compared with developments observed during the past few years, should not present a major financial problem to the economies of European countries. Difficulties of adjustment created by the ageing of the population should not, however, be underestimated; not only will the supply system have to meet the specific medical needs of an increasing number of old and very old people but the collective financing bodies will also have to cover services common to both the medical and social fields.

It is for this reason that in many countries special committees, of varying structures, have been set up to analyse the repercussions of the ageing of the population and have been entrusted, among other things, with proposing solutions and providing the necessary co-ordination. Some examples are the Swedish Parliamentary Commission on Ageing, set up in 1981, the work carried out since 1983 by the Steering Committee on Future Health Scenarios in the Netherlands and the working groups of the General Planning Commissariat in France. In the USSR both public opinion and government circles attached great importance to the setting up at the end of 1986 of the All Union Council for Veterans, whose role is not only to propose measures in favour of the elderly and to study their living conditions, but also to see to it that their specific needs are duly taken into account when overall economic and social policies are drawn up. Some countries have already adopted texts dealing specifically with the health of old people, such as Czechoslovakia in 1983 (Principal directives to improve the case of the elderly to 1990).

Similarly, many international organisations in addition to the ILO (the United Nations, the WHO, the IMF, the Council of Europe and the

ISSA) have recently produced reports and held meetings dealing with various aspects of the ageing of populations.

The distribution of health care to older persons

The introduction of any policy designed to meet the health needs of older persons must be preceded by an assessment of these needs, based both on the present situation and on assumptions upon which future projections can be made. The following factors should be taken into account:

— observation of the present situation shows that older people require more frequent medical treatment for the most common illnesses among the general population; furthermore, they represent a specific category owing to the chronic nature of their complaints and the fact that they suffer from various different illnesses at the same time, and may be disabled. Older persons should, therefore, together with the rest of the population, have access to all forms of medical treatment, medicines, surgery and rehabilitation programmes designed to cure their illnesses. Moreover, the attitude of older persons towards seeking medical treatment, their more frequent difficulties in carrying out the simplest everyday tasks and sometimes their isolation from family or society call for specific solutions in the fields of out-patient care, home care and institutional care;

— the medical consumption figures, as measured in various countries, provide the most reliable basis for projecting the frequency with which older persons can be expected to require various types of medical care; they cannot, however, be considered to represent standards which can be applied without some reservations;

— in attempting to determine the volume and nature of the appropriate means for meeting the future medical needs of older persons, assumptions should be based both on a critical assessment of the present situation (under- or over-consumption, the satisfactory or unsatisfactory distribution of out-patient care, home care and institutional care) and on conjectures as to the repercussions that social and technological change will have both on the nature of the demand for treatment and on the means of satisfying this demand.

In all countries, policies set out both to allow older people to stay as long as possible in their own homes and, whenever it is inevitable, to provide them with residential care in appropriate institutions. This approach not only complies with the wishes of those concerned, but is also in line with overall attempts to bring health expenditure under control by limiting recourse to hospitalisation as much as possible, since it is considered more expensive. There are various aspects to these policies: measures designed to prevent illnesses and disablement; action programmes in the fields of out-patient and home care; and adaptation of residential institutions faced with the prospect of the ageing of the population. On all these points, success depends on the introduction of adequate financial arrangements for staff training and for the development or adjustment of the working environment in general.

Prevention

It has already been pointed out that the use of a lower age limit to designate "old people" is merely a statistical device, used to define a sector of the population whose specific needs differ overall from those of younger age groups. The health needs of this older group are in fact more closely bound up with the number and nature of their complaints and handicaps than with age itself.

Faced with the foreseeable ageing of the population, health policies must naturally provide for ways of meeting needs that are undoubtedly going to increase; however, at the same time they should attempt, by preventive measures designed to delay the ageing process, to improve the quality of life at all ages and perhaps eventually to reduce these needs.

It may well be asked what the term "prevention" covers when it comes to ageing. The nature of diagnostic and health services, which might be considered preventive, changes over time as more is known about the influence of biological ageing and of disease on the health problems of older people.

Preventive measures differ from each other in several ways: the time in a person's life at which they are applied, the definition of the target populations, the medical and other means employed and their interaction with social and economic policies. One way to prevent deterioration in a person's health is to detect at an early stage, guard against, check and if possible treat any diseases that might affect him or her. Preventive measures of this type should be taken throughout a person's life and should concern older people, as well as the very young. They could be encouraged by introducing measures for collective financing, which is so often lacking.

The application of secondary preventive measures in the case of elderly people raises specific problems in so far as those concerned tend to underestimate their complaints and to put them down to age rather than to sickness, thereby delaying their recourse to the health system for treatment. Furthermore, medical personnel have not always been trained to recognise older people's illnesses, the symptoms of which are often less specific than those of younger people. Information and educational campaigns for both age groups could help to improve the situation.

The systematic implementation of tertiary preventive measures, which aim to reduce the consequences of illness, is particularly significant in the case of elderly people because of the relation between their present handicaps and the type of treatment that can be used for any subsequent illnesses.

A wide variety of measures outside the health sector, which aim at improving the everyday living conditions of older people, can also have beneficial effects on their health: these include economic measures to improve their standard of living, urban projects to help them move around more easily (e.g. ramps instead of staircases), adjustments to their homes so that they may be more independent in daily life, and the organisation of gymnastics courses and group cultural activities.

At this point, it is relevant to recall the specific preventive health policy adopted by many socialist countries to deal with the repercussions of ageing. This policy combines several original components, such as: the regular and systematic medical follow-up of persons approaching retire-ment age within the framework of occupational medicine; the adjustment of jobs and working hours to the abilities of ageing workers, on the basis of both general ergonomic studies and individual scientific tests; the possibility of rest cures in specialised institutions providing prophylactic treatment; and the regular follow-up at home by local health services of the health of older persons, to allow early diagnosis of any ailments. It is worth noting that these measures are in concordance with the spirit of the relevant provisions of the Older Workers Recommendation, 1980 (No. 162).

The various health-care sectors

As can be seen from the comparison between the medical con-sumption of older and young people, given earlier in this chapter, fewer adjustments will have to be made in the out-patient sector than in the fields of hospital and long-term institutional care. This would seem to be the most likely scenario, unless far-reaching social measures or new therapies make it possible to care for many more old people as out-patients rather than in hospital, or to keep them at home rather than placing them in institutions. This second prospect will be examined later.

According to estimates made for several countries in Europe, and by extension of the situation observed in France in 1980 (see table 33), persons over 65 years of age accounted in 1985, on average, for some 34 per cent of medical expenditure other than for long-term institutional

Table 33. Impact of ageing of populations on medical expenditure,[1] selected European countries, 1985, 2000 and 2015

Country	Per capita medical expenditure (index: Europe=100)			Average annual growth (%)[2]			% share of older persons in total expenditure					
							Over 65			Over 75		
	1985	2000	2015	1985–2000	2000–2015	1985–2015	1985	2000	2015	1985	2000	2015
Bulgaria	100	100	90	0.20	0.14	0.17	34	39	40	17	21	22
Czechoslovakia	98	96	95	0.07	0.25	0.16	33	32	38	18	18	18
Finland	100	101	105	0.29	0.50	0.39	33	36	45	18	20	22
German Dem. Rep.	102	102	103	0.22	0.29	0.26	36	39	42	23	19	24
Germany, Fed. Rep. of	104	106	107	0.37	0.34	0.35	37	42	45	22	22	27
Hungary	101	100	100	0.19	0.28	0.23	35	37	42	19	20	22
Ireland	93	89	88	−0.88	0.21	0.07	31	27	29	17	15	14
Sweden	106	106	107	0.19	0.31	0.25	42	41	47	23	25	26
Switzerland	107	113	114	0.58	0.36	0.47	40	46	53	22	26	32
Yugoslavia	94	95	98	0.28	0.48	0.38	26	35	39	14	17	20
Europe	100	100	100	0.21	0.27	0.24	34	37	41	19	20	22

[1] Calculations based on the following assumptions: United Nations population projections; differential growth rates, by age group, of average medical expenditure are those noted in France (INSEE/CREDES Inquiry, 1980) and are kept constant over the whole period.   [2] Growth due to changes in age structure.

care; in 2015 they will account for between 41 per cent (if the increase in expenditure per person remains the same according to age) and 58 per cent (if expenditure increases more rapidly in the case of old people, as has been observed in the past in France). For persons aged 75 years or over, it is estimated that the corresponding proportions in 2015 will be 22 and 32 per cent. Moreover, as far as the various types of health care are concerned, it is anticipated—the calculations being based only on the assumption of uniform growth—that in 2015 persons over 65 years of age will account for 14 per cent of expenditure on dentistry, 29 per cent on consultants, 40 per cent on general practitioners, 43 per cent on hospitalisation and 50 per cent on medicines. These estimates, which no doubt constitute minimum values, provoke reflection on changes in the activities of medical personnel and the need for corresponding training.

General practitioners, who are often the first contact a patient has with the health system when symptoms occur, have a particularly vital role to play in diagnosing, advising and providing follow-up for older persons. The increasing number of elderly people among their patients will gradually induce them to diversify their treatment and approach.

First of all, older persons take up much more of the doctor's time: not only do they require his or her services more frequently, but consultations usually last longer and often the doctor has to visit them at home. Consequently, a few more doctors will be needed to meet the demands of more or less the same number of people, but among whom will be an increasing proportion of older people.

The general practitioner is undoubtedly in the best position to recognise the first signs of an illness about which an older patient has not yet complained during a routine visit. To do this, he or she must be aware that illnesses in older patients may present different or less precise symptoms than in younger ones, and must be on the look-out when patients are confused or weak, a condition that might merely be put down to age, but which treatment could in fact check or even cure.

The introduction of district-based geriatric treatment in Czechoslovakia has already been mentioned. In the USSR the Institute of Gerontology of the Academy of Medical Sciences has drawn up special study programmes covering, for each medical speciality, the specific health problems of old people. The departments of gerontology at the Universities of Kiev and Leningrad provide special training for doctors responsible for the health care of old people in long-, medium- and short-stay establishments.

Decisions as to suitable treatment and its presentation, and advice to patients on healthy living habits, invariably impose on doctors a reflection which encompasses far more than the particular complaint being treated; older people usually suffer from a variety of ailments and often live in unfavourable conditions, which makes the doctor's task even more complicated. He or she has to decide which illness should be given priority, to take into account the fact that lack of mobility may make it difficult for the patient to attend for tests, to explain the treatment as simply as possible and to assess the chances of its being followed.

While great care must be taken when prescribing for old people a number of different pharmaceutical products to treat their multiple ailments—thus avoiding any adverse interactions—medicines prescribed in doses gauged according to the patient's weight are extremely important in maintaining physical and mental health in the elderly.

Older persons also account for an increasing percentage of the patients of other medical personnel. Nurses provide a wide range of health care at home; physiotherapists and speech therapists, among others, contribute towards rehabilitation in all its forms after accidents (fractures or strokes, for example). This type of therapy, which helps to mobilise all a person's faculties, is particularly important in geriatrics; being both curative and preventive, it enables many older people to remain independent or to become so once again.

In Eastern European countries special attention is also paid to what may be termed "social follow-up" for the elderly. Many youth organisations and other voluntary associations undertake to visit and assist old people living in their neighbourhoods. The elderly are very often active in their own clubs or associations. Moreover, retired persons continue, so to speak, to form part of their former enterprises and to benefit from many privileges, ranging from the provision of meals to home repairs carried out by the enterprise. In the German Democratic Republic retired workers' trade associations are responsible for seeing to it that the interests of pensioners—particularly as regards social and cultural services—are taken into account in the negotiation of enterprise agreements. The following figures are taken from the WHO inquiry mentioned earlier: in Bucharest the proportion of men and women between the ages of 65 and 74 who had received help in their homes in the previous 12 months was of the order of 50 per cent, whereas in Western European countries it was less than 10 per cent, with the exception of Tampere (Finland) where the figure was, however, still under 30 per cent.[22] There can be no doubt that such practices help considerably in conserving the health of old people, it being generally agreed that the affective and social surroundings are very often the deciding factor.

It is obviously very important to co-ordinate medical personnel dispensing out-patient and home care for older persons in order to ensure the continuity of treatment given to patients who may find it more difficult than others to transmit information from doctors to medical auxiliaries.

The hospital sector has been developed and brought up to date in European countries during the past few years, especially during the 1970s. Not only does a hospital accommodate the sick who need to stay in to be treated; it is also the place where specialised and technical out-patient care is being developed and dispensed. These changes have been accompanied by an increase in the number and diversity of hospital staff, with a concomitant rise in hospital expenditure, which has grown much more rapidly than other health costs.

Within the context of these technical changes, and in an attempt to rationalise the treatment dispensed in order to bring rising health expenditure under control, all countries are having second thoughts about the number of older people in hospitals; they are wondering whether persons aged 65 years or over, who account for about one-third of hospital patients receiving short- and medium-term care, might not get a better reception and treatment in establishments which are more geared to their actual needs and are less expensive.

There is no doubt that older persons who, on average, are financially worse off than the rest of the population and tend to live more alone and in less favourable conditions, have benefited, more than other age groups, from the hospital's traditional role of taking in patients. In their case, hospital has presented an alternative to other forms of treatment, closed to them for financial reasons or because there was not enough room in appropriate institutions. Policy-makers are now attempting to find solutions to replace hospitalisation: nursing homes are one possibility and they will be dealt with later in the text. However, policies setting out to reduce the number of older persons entering hospital should bear in mind that disabilities and chronic de-generative diseases are only a part of their clinical state and that in some cases there might be both psychological and economic advantages to hospitalisation.

It should be stressed that the treatment given to older persons in short-stay establishments has changed over the years and covers new needs. Improved methods of diagnosis and treatment and the decline in certain prejudices on the frailness of the elderly have opened up new possibilities, and old people are now treated more actively in hospitals than in the past. Progress made in anaesthetics and resuscitation techniques have made it possible to carry out operations on old and very old people under better conditions, whether these operations are "tra-ditional" or ultra-modern, such as coronary bypasses, artificial hips, and so on. These operations, combined with rehabilitation, can contribute greatly to making certain old persons independent again, thereby enabling them to stay at home and delaying their need for institutional care.

Long-term treatment

It is in the field of long-term care that the foreseeable ageing of the population, by greatly increasing needs, presents a real challenge to decision-makers.[23]

To degrees that differ in each country, long-term care is dispensed either in a wide variety of long-stay institutions, in which the stress placed on medical facilities or amenities also varies, or in the patient's home. Among the former are general hospitals, psychiatric hospitals and various types of convalescent home; residential premises may be collective (old people's homes, sheltered housing) or individual (private homes). A fairly wide range of staff helps to dispense care or to assist old people in their everyday existence: doctors, paramedical staff, social workers, and household and family helpers.

Nursing homes are a vital component of any health care programme for older people: however, depending on the role that the decision-makers wish to assign to them in the health and welfare system, objectives as to the required capacity and quality of these institutions vary considerably. These differences arise because, according to the country and period in time, varying emphasis is placed on possibilities of transferring hospital patients from general and psychiatric hospitals to medically supervised institutions or on measures enabling disabled patients to remain at home and avoid having to stay for a long time in an institution. In fact, the admission of patients to various types of establishments is not strictly related to their degree of disablement or health needs: the extreme differences in the state of health of patients in institutions show only too well that other criteria, such as availability and proximity, the family environment and financial resources, often play a decisive role.

Definitions of categories of establishment vary and make international comparisons difficult; however, it would seem that the proportion of older people entering institutions differs considerably from country to country. For example, the rate among those over the age of 65 is just above 1 per cent in Yugoslavia, 4 per cent in the Federal Republic of Germany, 8.1 per cent in the Netherlands and 10 per cent in Sweden. In all countries the rates are higher for women and increase rapidly after the age of 75; they are, for instance, 31 per cent for persons over the age of 80 in Sweden and 40 per cent among those over the age of 85 in the Netherlands. Recent developments appear to show that the age of resident patients is rising and that the social and financial reasons for sending them to long-term institutions are giving way to medical reasons: this results in an increased demand for skilled staff and for equipment in such establishments.[24]

Alongside solutions proposing permanent institutional care there are, depending on the country, various forms of long-term treatment which might be termed intermediary because they combine out-patient care and institutional care. These may include day care in nursing homes (the Netherlands), out-patient departments in psychiatric hospitals, regular care provided by district nurses and paid or voluntary teams of home helps. In the USSR a recent government decree aims to develop the construction of residential apartments specifically geared to the needs of elderly persons.

Finally, much of the long-term treatment and support given to older people in everyday life is provided at home by the patient's family, friends and neighbours. It is because of this factor, as a United Nations report on ageing in the world has pointed out, that the percentage of persons aged 65 years of age and over living in institutions does not exceed 7 per cent in Europe.[25]

In all the discussion on the subject of ageing populations, emphasis is placed on the medical, social and financial advantages of each of the various forms of care in relation to the type of illness to be treated, the desires of the elderly themselves and the financial constraints involved. As already mentioned, all countries aim to keep older people in their home environment for as long as possible; this is combined with the objective of providing residential care, if required, in suitable conditions. Increased capacity, proper staff training and appropriate techniques should be used to help patients to switch from one type of treatment to another whenever this seems feasible and desirable; provisions on coverage and general financing should aim to make this easier.

Paradoxically, the literature on the subject gives many examples of the inadequacy of hospital living conditions and care to meet the needs of their older patients, at the same time stressing the shortage of accommodation (especially in psychiatric institutions) and the efforts made by various countries to remedy this state of affairs.

Attempts to improve and increase amenities have been made by Belgium, France, the German Democratic Republic and Sweden: during the past few years, these countries have applied policies to provide medical supervision in existing structures and to build new establishments for elderly sick persons. These policies attempt to meet the needs of an ever-growing older population and to cut down on the number of old persons entering short- and medium-stay establishments and general and psychiatric hospitals.

In France the old people's wards in public hospitals, which previously served only to provide very basic accommodation for elderly patients have gradually been transformed. Some have become old people's homes and others provide long-stay medical care.

In Belgium there are geriatric services for the intensive care of very old persons run by a physician who specialises in internal medicine; "*Services-V*" provide long-term treatment for older persons with the prospect of returning to their home environment; "*Services-R*" set out to rehabilitate patients by active means; and, finally, neuropsychiatric services provide hospital treatment for patients suffering from serious behavioural disorders. In practice, however, the patients treated in these "services" are not always those for whom, theoretically, they were originally intended.

In Sweden much emphasis is placed on the lack of accommodation in such institutions, even though the avowed intention is to maintain old people in their usual living environments as long as possible. The number of hospital beds for the chronically ill has been considerably increased, new nursing homes with more amenities have been built and county councils are planning to increase still further the capacity of long-stay institutions providing medical treatment.

In the German Democratic Republic the number of places available in long-stay establishments gradually increased from 29 per 1,000 residents of pensionable age in 1971 to 45 per 1,000 in 1983. At the same time, an ambitious programme of purpose-built accommodation for old people, designed to enable them to lead an independent existence as long as possible, has been undertaken.

Alongside the increase in medically supervised long-term establishments and the development of new forms of out-patient care or home care for older persons, there is a need for staff of varying skills. Staff training is a central component of present policy; however, there are different approaches to this problem, depending on the country, with contradictory views as to whether geriatrics should or should not be considered a special branch of medicine. In the United Kingdom it is rapidly developing as a special field; in Denmark long-term care has been considered a separate branch of medicine since 1972. Reference has already been made to the slightly different attitude adopted in the USSR. In Finland and Norway the treatment of old people requires additional qualifications, for nurses as well as for doctors. In spite of the efforts undertaken, medical staff and social workers as a whole must be made more aware of the problems of ageing.

Over the past few decades, improvements in medical techniques in all countries have greatly improved the outlook for the diagnosis and treatment of disease: together with the development of collective coverage of medical expenses, they have contributed to the growth of medical consumption, and have helped to improve health standards and bring down mortality rates; but they have also been a factor in the rising cost of medical treatment. Nevertheless, not all technical innovations lead to increased expenditure; their impact differs according to their nature (pharmaceuticals, sophisticated apparatus), field of application, ease or difficulty of implementation, cost, and the benefits they are expected to bring: new cures, fewer after-effects and less risk of relapse, greater safety of treatment and increased comfort for the patient.

At this point, mention should of course be made of the results achieved in Romania, by the Aslan Institute, with products designed to combat ageing such as Gerovital H3. Similarly, in the USSR, the Institute of Gerontology in Kiev, alongside its programme of ergological, biological and pharmacological research, has produced a number of foodstuffs designed particularly for older persons.

At all these levels, it would seem, from the above indicators, that older people have benefited in the past from advances in medicine; recent progress and current research point to a continuation along these lines, social policies permitting; however, the conflicting repercussions that can be expected from various technical innovations and their impact on medical expenditure may greatly influence the choices that will be made. In some cases, new techniques are a source of additional expenditure if they enable treatment to be extended to persons previously considered too weak to undergo it on grounds of safety (surgery for older people, for example), if they keep illnesses under control and keep people alive, provided they undergo constant treatment (certain medicines) or if they provide a better quality of life (physiotherapy).

On the other hand, certain technical innovations can cut costs in treatment and be just as effective, either because they themselves are cheaper or because they allow other types of treatment to be substituted. For instance, older persons will certainly benefit from progress in the field of lasers and optic fibres, which make it possible to avoid or shorten the usual stay in hospital for various surgical operations (e.g. for cataracts). On another level, new forms of communication and electronic controls might make it easier for older people to stay at home. Denmark appears to be making a special effort in this field by installing increasingly sophisticated home alarm systems linked to mobile security services where professional staff are on hand to answer calls.

Research is being undertaken in several countries on biological ageing and ways to prevent and cure certain illnesses associated with old age such as Alzheimer's disease (senile dementia), osteoporosis and metabolic illnesses. By 2015 the findings might give rise to new bio-medical technologies, overturn ways of treating certain diseases and alter the cost. Thus, it is reasonable to assume that the advanced research under way at the Soviet Institute of Gerontology and in scientific institutions in other European countries may, before long, completely transform the traditional approach to illness and hence to the social integration of the old and the very old.

The financing of health care

Because the burden of medical expenditure tends to fall more heavily on some than on others, and in a desire to provide equal access to medical care for all, collective coverage has now become the rule: it spreads over a greater number of people the financial risks associated with the onset of illness, which could place an intolerable strain on the individual budget. Depending on the country, collective coverage is provided either by statutory health insurance bodies set up especially for the purpose, or by the State and regional or local communities acting in the name of "solidarity". The funds for coverage of medical expenses may be drawn from wage earners' and employers' contributions or may be financed out of tax revenue, as mentioned in the first part of this chapter.

As long as economic growth was sustained, the policy of maintaining or, sometimes, increasing the share of collective financing in health expenditure posed no major problems, even though this expenditure was growing more rapidly than the economy as a whole. Over the past few years, however, the worsening economic climate in many European countries, coupled with rising unemployment, has made it increasingly difficult to finance social expenditure. Since the contribution base is also growing more slowly, there are now only two ways of maintaining the same level of coverage: the first is to increase compulsory deductions and allow social expenditure to continue rising rapidly; the second is to try to limit the growth of expenditure in order to avoid increasing deductions. This latter solution seems to prevail in many countries, although its advantages and disadvantages in the short and medium term are seen differently by the social partners in social, political and economic terms.

In this context, some decision-makers view the demographic prospects in Europe as a factor impeding their efforts to bring down movements in social expenditure to the level of the economy as a whole in an attempt to balance the resources and expenditure of the social services. On the one hand, the ageing of the population, added to the introduction of early retirement schemes, is bringing about a decline in the proportion of economically active persons in the total population, that is, of the very people on whom the contributions needed to finance social services are levied. At the same time, high unemployment rates also narrow the field for deduction of contributions to social security systems.

On the other hand, if legislation remains unchanged, the rise in the number of older persons will result both in an increase in the cost of statutory age-related benefits such as pensions, and in higher demand for such benefits as the coverage of medical consumption, which usually increases with age.

Nevertheless, the role generally assigned to the ageing of the population in the growth of health expenditure is often exaggerated. As already discussed, it has been calculated that changes in the age pyramid cannot alone account for more than a small portion of the growth of medical expenditure observed in the past, and that the same holds good for the future. Demographic changes will have far less impact on the health sector than on retirement pensions; however, since the desire to limit compulsory deductions involves both sectors and since the former, apparently at least, lends itself better to adjustments, it seems that the option of bringing health expenditure under control partly reflects the difficulties encountered in financing the cost of retirement pensions, whose growth appears to be inevitable.

Social welfare systems, through their manner of collecting funds and distributing benefits, operate transfers of resources between subgroups of the population. Of course, if legislation remains unchanged, demographic changes are bound to have an influence here and, therefore, on the extent and the nature of solidarity between social classes or between population groups. In the health sector, the increase in the number of older persons calls for greater solidarity between generations and the transfer of a growing share of labour income to persons who are unlikely to participate in the productive sector again or whose further participation is, for physiological reasons, likely to be fairly brief. In assessing the relationship between economic growth and rising medical expenditure, the negative repercussions should be weighed against the positive ones that the extension of the medical sector has on a country's economy: job creation, technological development, and so on.

In spite of this, taking the stand that the increase in medical expenditure might be an obstacle to economic development, many countries have, since 1975, taken a wide range of measures to bring this expenditure under control. These have included an increase in the financial participation of patients for certain types of treatment, control over the way care is dispensed and revised payment policies. It seems that these steps have, at least in part, contributed towards the decline of the growth rates in medical expenditure which have been observed during the past few years in the countries in question.[26]

The level of social protection in the health field is the outcome of inter-relations between a number of technical, economic, social and political factors on both a national and an international scale, and there is no knowing how these factors will evolve over the next 30 years. It is, however, conceivable that, over the next decade, economic constraints will continue to hamper the pursuit of ambitious social welfare plans involving increased collective coverage of medical expenditure. It is even possible that a number of countries will continue their policies of controlling expenditure—not only the expenditure financed from social security funds but medical expenditure in its entirety. In fact, the negotiations at which ways and means of covering the cost of medical treatment are discussed, and which provide collective financing bodies with an opportunity to propose such prices and rates of coverage as will enable them to meet their expenditure on medical benefits, can also be used to introduce financial curbs on increases in the volume of medical consumption.

Older persons are concerned both by the rules on financial coverage, whether generous or restrictive, which apply to all medical care and by those, more selective, that affect either their demographic group or certain types of medical treatment which they require more frequently than younger people and which account for a large part of their medical consumption.

In many countries special provisions have been adopted for older people, making it easier for them to receive certain types of medical treatment, even if provision for other types of therapy, considered to be at the limit between medical and social care, is inadequate. For example:

— in the United Kingdom general practitioners, who are paid a fixed amount per patient, receive a higher fee for those over 65 years of age, which encourages them to take on older persons;

— in the Netherlands, whereas statutory health insurance covers persons under the age of 65 only if their incomes are below a certain limit, medical insurance used to be available to all persons over that age without exception; however, the country's economic difficulties have recently led to the withdrawal of this arrangement;

— in Yugoslavia older persons are considered in laws and regulations to belong to one of the three "vulnerable" groups of the population (together with mothers—present and future—and children) and thereby benefit from special health care provisions;

— in countries where patients are generally expected to make a financial contribution towards certain medical costs, older persons are often exempted either because of their age (for example, medicines and spectacles in the United Kingdom, medicines purchased in pharmacies for several categories of retired persons in the USSR), or because, most of the time, they fulfil the necessary requirements such as low income, high medical expenses, protracted illness, and so on.

As was seen earlier, old persons are more likely than younger ones to suffer concurrently from a number of pathological states, from chronic illness and from disabilities requiring ongoing treatment. Moreover, they often live in straitened financial circumstances or are cut off from family and society; this can hamper both access to care and its distribution. When older persons are patients in the long-stay wards of hospitals and other institutions, this is often for social as well as medical reasons and the two may be difficult to dissociate. Regulations on the financing of long-term care, which are usually far less generous than those for hospitalisation, (often provided free of charge for short- and medium-stay patients), reflect this duality.

The fact is that, although legislation is far from uniform in the countries under study, the social services often cover only part of the cost of institutional accommodation and care. The patient has to make a contribution, which can either be standard (as in the Netherlands for stays of over six months), calculated on the basis of a means test (Denmark, Sweden), established as a lump sum, or designed to cover the expenses for accommodation but not medical care itself (Belgium, France). The amount owed by the patients may be deducted from their pensions, their other sources of income or even from their assets (Norway). In the USSR older persons living in "residences" (long-term establishments partially under medical supervision) hand over from 75 to 90 per cent of their pensions in exchange for full maintenance, including clothing. Sometimes, however, the State and the local communities provide additional funds either in the form of subsidies to the establishment or by assistance to the individual. As already mentioned, the bodies responsible for paying pensions may help to finance the care required by their recipients in their own areas, either in total (Yugoslavia) or in part (Federal Republic of Germany, Luxembourg).

Differences in financial regulations can in some cases lead to older persons being admitted to hospitals whereas, in fact, their state of health would rather justify their being placed in a long-term establishment, which is usually less expensive; however, given the present economic situation and the prospect of an increase in the number of older persons, it is extremely unlikely that the financial coverage of institutional care will be increased.

It might well be asked whether financial provisions encouraging the interchangeability of various forms of treatment might not both better meet the needs of older persons and restrict the growth of medical expenditure in the future. These could naturally include various measures to encourage the development of preventive health programmes or home care, or to enable the patient to be placed in the most suitable long-term institution. In addition, there is the problem of how the relevant financial coverage should be shared between the State, the local community, health insurance bodies, other social welfare organisations and the family.

No more will be said about the fact that preventive care is usually inadequately covered by health insurance bodies, a situation which is necessarily different in countries where the entity financing and dispensing medical care is one and the same, such as those with a national health service. Nevertheless, even in countries which have such a system, there is no uniformity with regard to preventive care; even when a national health service is in operation, it is clear that for both national policies and preventive measures to be truly effective, responsibility for the latter must devolve on independent bodies within the public health service. In any event, efforts in this field in respect of all ages could perhaps lead to savings in the long or medium term, and would certainly have beneficial effects on the health and quality of life of elderly people. In the short term, however, such measures cannot be expected to reduce the need for financing of medical care.[27]

Provisions to encourage older people to stay at home could take several forms: out-patient and home care could be made more comprehensive; certain welfare services (home helps, "meals on wheels", etc.) could be financially covered; allowances could be made available to families and voluntary neighbourhood associations; and subsidies could be granted to improve fittings in homes and to install modern communications equipment. In the same way that health insurance has encouraged the development and widespread use of new methods of diagnosis and treatment, so might an increase in public financing for the home care of older persons prompt new technological developments to make it easier to keep old and disabled persons in their home environment.

Although, from a health and humanitarian point of view, trends in this direction might seem desirable, their financial repercussions are far less obvious: first, taking care of older persons at home is not necessarily cheaper than looking after them in an institution; second, provisions made to substitute one form of treatment for another do not always have the desired effect.

The question of the cost of home care relative to institutional care can be viewed in different ways, depending upon whether account is taken only of the expenses incurred by welfare organisations or also of the advantages involved in both solutions from the point of view of the old person's morale; it also depends on whether care provided on an informal basis by members of the family and neighbours is given a financial value, and what value. If care provided by the family, which bears the greatest burden in caring for patients at home, is considered as "free", there can be no doubt that, at present, home care is much cheaper than institutional care. If, however, in the future most of the nursing care at home were to be carried out by paid professionals, the economic aspect of this problem would be quite different. The findings of studies carried out on this subject do not always agree.

According to a Canadian report, the cost of treating an illness at home is the same as that of hospital treatment, for the same illness for the same length of time.[28] A recent ISSA report on long-term care even goes as far as to say that the expense of providing long-term home care equal in intensity to care in an institution would be prohibitive.[29] On the other side, a Belgian report concludes that home care costs less, except for persons requiring constant attention.[30] A Swiss report also pleads in favour of home care, not only for humanitarian reasons but also because the cost is only one-third of that of institutional treatment.[31]

When assessing the financial repercussions of a policy to keep elderly sick people at home, it is not enough merely to compare costs for institutional and home care. Keeping more people at home—first and foremost those who are least ill and least disabled—might indirectly affect the overall cost of institutional care because institutions would have a higher proportion of seriously ill people requiring more care. Furthermore, as needs for institutional care in many countries are far from being met at present, it is likely that the development of home care would tend to supplement rather than replace this form of treatment.

The choice between the various possible ways of accommodating older people needing medical treatment must take into account such factors as the proximity of the establishment, the nature of the services offered and the waiting time for admission. It is also influenced by the financial coverage available. Greater uniformity in the coverage of hospital care and care in other institutions would, in many European countries, avoid a situation in which patients choose to go to hospital rather than to another type of establishment more for financial than for medical reasons.

The expected growth of medical expenditure in general and the increasing financial difficulties of the social services have led some countries to consider cutting public health coverage. If such policies were to prevail, and even if the measures taken applied to the population as a whole, it is likely that older people, who need medical care most but usually have fewer financial resources, would be affected more than the others. For example:

— measures which seen globally might appear minor, such as cuts in the reimbursement rates of certain medicines or the establishment of flat-rate payments for hospital care introduced in several countries, could make it financially difficult for older people to seek treatment;

— the financing of hospitals from an overall budget, which is now the rule in many countries, is likely to result in older people leaving hospital early to enter other institutions, or in their hospital stays being divided up into shorter periods, with all the disadvantages this involves both medically and from the point of view of the patients' morale;

— older people could not fail to be in a position of inferiority if certain plans to restore or develop market economy regulatory machinery in the health sector were to be implemented in Europe. Leaving the choice of an insurance fund and of the level of coverage up to individuals, which in principle is designed to make them stand on their own feet, means little in the case of people at high risk and with low incomes.

As regards long-term care, the multiplicity and fragmented nature of sources of funding seem ill-adapted to the needs of older people for whom medical and non-medical fields overlap. Where they exist, health insurance schemes usually cover only medical consumption; the State and the local communities step in to provide additional social services. Those services which are not thus covered are provided on a voluntary basis by various charitable organisations, the family and neighbours.

In view of the predicted increase in the number of older persons during the coming years, the problem arises of who is going to cover the corresponding increase in medical and social expenditure. Although slight when compared with medical expenditure for the population as a whole, this increase nevertheless represents additional costs which have to be met in a difficult economic climate. In many countries it is believed that the introduction of new forms of home treatment might be able to rely upon the development of voluntary work, thus reducing public financing needs. This trend towards another form of solidarity between generations would be encouraged by reducing working hours and early retirement. However, is it truly realistic to expect more from this voluntary work than a mere substitution of services at present rendered by families which, in time, can only be on the decline with the drop in the number of children per family and the changing pattern of family life in general?

*

*　　　*

In many fields, economic and social policy-makers have to take decisions on future action, even though they may find it difficult to grasp thoroughly the present situation and to foresee future trends. The same goes for the care of older persons, but in this case, at least, one thing is certain: their number is going to increase in future years and account must be taken of this factor when planning how treatment is to be dispensed and financed.

Admittedly, it is more difficult to estimate needs in health care and social services, which reflect morbidity rates and the technological level and living conditions of a given period; however, even in this case, the uncertainties are not unduly great. In examining past trends, it can reasonably be predicted, given the extent of needs not met until now in spite of attempts at rationalisation, that medical expenditure on the whole will continue to rise during the next few years and that older people will account for an increasing proportion of it. If elderly persons do not become the target of restrictive policies, this proportion should, on average, in Europe, be close to 50 per cent in 2015; it will be higher for institutional care and lower for services provided by consultants. Only considerable advances in the war against the major diseases associated with old age could overturn these forecasts, by lowering the costs of certain types of treatment or enabling economic choices to be made between different forms of care and accommodation.

The economic and social climate is hardly propitious for the development of collective public financing of health expenditure as a whole, which is sometimes considered, perhaps wrongly, to be non-productive; neither does it lend itself to increased solidarity between generations. Nevertheless, among those who are or will be old between 1985 and 2015, there are many who will have contributed during their working lives to the great economic progress experienced in Europe after the Second World War; they can claim every right to benefit in their turn from the widespread social welfare systems they have helped to set up. However, those at work today, from whose wages deductions are made to finance social services, will not willingly accept an increase in their contributions unless the way in which the needs of old people are met shows them that their present financial efforts are an investment for later years. In each country the ability to cope with problems raised by the ageing of the population is, in this respect, a test for the future of social systems.

Notes

[1] See in particular P. Mouton: "Analyse comparée des systèmes de santé", in *Futuribles* (Paris), Oct.–Nov. 1985, pp. 53–71.

[2] For a more detailed description of the case of the Federal Republic of Germany, see Ch. 3, p. 92.

[3] John W. Rowe: "Health care of the elderly", in *New England Journal of Medicine* (Waltham, Massachusetts), Vol. 312, No. 13, p. 830.

⁴ Thérèse Lecomte: *Evolution de la morbidité déclarée—France 1970–1980*, CREDES report (Paris, Mar. 1986), p. 35.

⁵ In the Federal Republic of Germany in 1978, the proportion of persons suffering from chronic diseases was 13.5 per cent under the age of 15 and 33.1 per cent for those between 40 and 50 years of age, reaching 84.9 per cent at 65 years of age and over (F. J. Oldiges: "Long-term care of the elderly and disabled in the Federal Republic of Germany", in ISSA: *Long-term care and social security*, Studies and Research No. 21 (Geneva, 1984), pp. 106–116.

⁶ The Netherlands, Steering Committee on Future Health Scenarios: *Growing old in the future* (Dordrecht, Martinus Nijhoff, 1987), p. 194. Rowe, op. cit., reports a frequency of 2.5 per cent for serious dementia among persons aged 65 and over, plus 10 per cent suffering from mild dementia. In France in 1981, 13.1 per cent of hospital patients over the age of 65 suffered from dementia (C. Sermet: *Les personnes âgées à l'hôpital*, CREDES report (Paris, 1st quarter 1987), p. 67.

⁷ A. M. Davies: "Epidemiology and the challenge of ageing", in *International Journal of Epidemiology* (Oxford), Vol. 14, No. 1, Mar. 1985, pp. 9–19; Henri Pequinot: "Y a-t-il un grand âge?", in *La Revue hospitalière de France*, No. 377, Jan. 1985, pp. 10–17; Sweden, National Commission on Aging: *Just another age*, A Swedish report to the World Assembly on Aging, 1982 (Stockholm, 1982), p. 16.

⁸ The Netherlands, Steering Committee on Future Health Scenarios: *Growing old in the future*, op. cit., p. 92.

⁹ Pierre-Alain Audirac: "Les personnes âgées, de la vie de famille à l'isolement", in *Economie et Statistique* (Paris, INSEE), No. 175, Mar. 1985, pp. 39–54.

¹⁰ K. G. Wright: *Economic aspects of strategies for the health care of the elderly*, Report prepared for the European Office of the World Health Organization (York, University of York, Centre for Health Economics, 1986; mimeographed), p. 162.

¹¹ Information received by the ILO directly from the governments concerned.

¹² Lecomte, op. cit., and An. and Ar. Mizrahi: "Evaluation de l'état de santé des personnes âgées en France, à l'aide de plusieurs indicateurs", in *Revue d'Epidémiologie et de Santé publique* (Paris), No. 29, 1981, p. 443.

¹³ WHO, Regional Office for Europe: *The elderly in eleven countries: A sociomedical survey*, Public Health in Europe 21 (Copenhagen, 1983).

¹⁴ Henri Pequignot: "Y a-t-il un grand âge?", in *La vie en plus*, Colloquium organised by the International Centre of Social Gerontology, Rome, 1984 (Paris, 1986), p. 192; also published in *La Revue hospitalière de France*, No. 377, Jan. 1985.

¹⁵ An. and Ar. Mizrahi: "Invalidité et variables socio-démographiques", in *Handicaps et inadaptations, Les cahiers du CTNERHI*, No. 29, Jan.–Mar. 1985, pp. 33–43.

¹⁶ INSEE-CREDOC Inquiries, 1970 and 1980. Findings analysed and published mainly by INSEE and CREDES.

¹⁷Alan Maynard: "Aspects économiques des soins aux personnes âgées en Grande-Bretagne", in France. Commissariat général du Plan: *Systèmes de santé, pouvoirs publics et financeurs: qui contrôle quoi?*, Proceedings of an international conference on health policies, Paris, March 1985 (Paris, la Documentation française, 1987), pp. 71–83; Peter S. Heller et als.: *Aging and social expenditures in the major industrial countries, 1980–2025* (Washington, DC, IMF, 1986); Ministry of Social affairs and Health: *Aging in Finland*, Finnish National Report for the World Assembly on Aging (Helsinki, 1982).

¹⁸ George J. Schieber (in *Delivering health care in the OECD: Past, present and future*, Paper prepared for a meeting, "Health and Pensions Policies in the Context of Demographic and Economic Constraints", Tokyo, 25–28 November 1985) shows that, between 1960 and 1983, health expenditure increased in real terms by an average of 6.2 per cent per annum for a group of seven OECD countries. More recently (1975–83) growth was slower at an annual average rate of 3.3 per cent. See, for *France*, An. and Ar. Mizrahi and S. Sandier: "Les facteurs démographiques et la croissance des consommations médicales", in *Consommation* (Paris), No. 1, 1974, p. 30; for the *United Kingdom*, Maynard, op. cit.; for *Sweden*, Bengt Jonsson: *The influence on health care expenditures of changes in population age structure*, IHE Report (in this study it is calculated that between 1980 and 2010, with uniform growth, the effect on ageing would lead to an annual increase of 0.36 per cent in total medical expenditure in Sweden); for the *Federal Republic of Germany*, Bundesminister für Arbeit und Sozialordnung: "Auswirkungen der Bevölkerungsentwicklung auf Leistungsnachfrage und Ausgaben im Gesundheitswesen—insbesondere der gesetzlichen Krankenversicherung—unter Berücksichtigung von Zielvorstellungen über die Gesundheitsversorgung ältere Menschen", in *Forschungsbericht, Gesundheitsforschung*, No. 95, p. 215; and for the *United States*, Louise B. Russel: *An aging population and the use of medical care*, Brookings General Series Reprint 370 (Washington, DC, The Brookings Institution, 1981). This study shows that the ageing of the

population in the United States between 1985 and 2015 would lead to an annual increase of 0.3 per cent in hospital admissions and a rise of 0.8 per cent in the number of nursing home patients in the total population, with the number of visits to doctors and dentists remaining more or less unchanged.

[19] IMF: *Aging and social expenditures in the major industrial countries, 1980–2025* (Washington, DC, Sep. 1986).

[20] Calculations based on 1970–80 French data show that, on the assumptions of differential growth rates for the various age groups, and a constant age structure of the population, there would be additional growth in medical expenditure of 0.023 per cent per annum. This is to say that, over a ten-year period, if the growth rate were zero to begin with (medical consumption per head remaining unchanged over the first two years), during the second year it would be 0.023 per cent, during the third year 0.046 per cent, and in the last year 0.2 per cent.

[21] Calculations based on 1970–80 French data show, for instance, that, assuming that the differential growth rates of the various age groups remain unchanged, and if the objective were to stabilise the average volume of medical consumption per head, there would be a drop in medical consumption for persons between 5 and 39 years of age. With less strict containment of medical consumption—i.e. if it were to rise by an annual average of 2 per cent—the medical consumption of the 5–19 year-old group would have to fall. The average annual growth rate would need to be over 3.7 per cent if consumption levels were to be maintained for all age groups.

[22] See WHO: *The elderly in eleven countries*, op cit., table 52.

[23] The comments which follow are in part based on study findings published by the International Social Security Association (ISSA). See in particular: *Long-term care and social security*, Studies and Research No. 21 (Geneva, 1984), and *Long-term care for the elderly provided within the framework of health care schemes*, Report submitted to the XXIInd General Assembly, Montreal, 1986 (mimeographed).

[24] See in particular Dorothy P. Rice: "Long-term eare of the elderly and the disabled", in ISSA: *Long-term care and social security*, op. cit., pp. 1–34; Wright, op. cit. the Netherlands, Steering Committee on Future Health Scenarios: *Growing old in the future*, op. cit., p. 92.

[25] United Nations: *The world aging situation: Strategies and policies* (New York, 1985).

[26] OECD: *Measuring health care 1960–83: Expenditure, costs and performance* (Paris, 1985).

[27] Simone Sandier: "Accès, qualité et efficacité: soins dispensés par les médecins, les pharmaciens et les autres services ambulatoires", in *Les politiques de santé et de retraite face aux contraintes économiques et démographiques*, Proceedings of an OECD conference, Tokyo, November 1985 (Paris, OECD; forthcoming).

[28] Study by Gerson and Hughes, quoted by Rice, op. cit., p. 29.

[29] ISSA: *Long-term care for the elderly provided within the framework of health care schemes*, op. cit., p. 21.

[30] Wright, op. cit., "Belgium", pp. 60–67.

[31] P. Gilliand: "Domiciliary care: A partial alternative to institutionalisation", in ISSA: *Long-term care and social security*, op. cit., pp. 150–158. On this subject, see also a French report, D. Coudreau: "The French system of domiciliary care for the elderly", ibid.

BY WAY OF CONCLUSION

5

It can be seen from the preceding chapters that demographic developments are only one of many aspects of the problems affecting social security. In concluding this study, it would seem worth while to recall, in general terms, some of the ways in which demographic constraints are expected to influence the future of social protection in Europe. To use accounting terms, there are two sides to the problems faced by social security: the "credit" side, which covers the economically active members of the population, those who pay contributions and taxes and in so doing generate the resources needed to run the system; and the "debit" side, consisting of the subpopulations requiring support, in other words, the beneficiaries, i.e. children, the unemployed, the sick and pensioners.

THE CREDIT SIDE: HUMAN RESOURCES

The working-age population in Europe will increase slightly in the best of cases, remain stable or even decline a little over the next 40 years. Above all, however, its demographic structure is showing signs of an internal change which will become more pronounced in that the number of persons aged 40 years and over is going to equal and then outnumber the 20- to 39-year-old age group. This is in total contradiction to the "natural" demographic structure, i.e. a structure in which neither fertility nor mortality rates have been brought under control, as is still the case for the majority of the world population. In this respect, European populations, together with those of several non-European industrialised countries, have characteristics which clearly set them apart from the rest of the world.

Instead of suffering from a labour "scarcity" due to an excessively young demographic structure, European populations undergoing change have an exceptionally high number of persons aged between 20 and 59

163

years, at a time when the young population is falling off and the population aged 60 years and over has not yet increased to the extent expected after the year 2000. This vast human potential would be an asset if it were not affected by long-lasting unemployment which is neither cyclical nor frictional. Wherever unemployment statistics exist, they show that nearly 10 per cent of the working-age population have no job and therefore constitute another population group requiring support, whether or not they are covered by social security schemes. These unemployed persons constitute a large "reservoir" of labour which could, at least to begin with, be tapped to offset the effects of demographic ageing.

At the same time, it might be thought that a decline in population could bring about a noticeable fall in unemployment. This is not the place to go into the substance of the problem—which is an extraordinarily complex one—but it should not be forgotten that it is of capital importance to social security programmes. High unemployment rates lead both to a drop in receipts and to a rise in expenditure. It is not, however, certain that a fall in the numbers of the actively employed in the countries of Europe will lead to a corresponding drop in the number of jobseekers. In fact, unemployment has been shown to vary widely according to sex, age, occupational branch, skills and wage levels. In any one region there may be considerable unemployment in one sector and a manpower shortage in another. Transfer from the depressed sector to the understaffed sector is always difficult and rarely happens to any great extent, since jobs and skills are not interchangeable.

A small part of unemployment is frictional, part is residual and yet another part is cyclical, but the great majority of those who are unemployed today are the victims of the radical changes that are unsettling the economic apparatus of industrialised societies which, although they have already achieved a high level of productivity, must raise it still further to meet the challenge of foreign competition.

Despite the slowing down of population growth it is, then, unrealistic to expect an automatic fall in unemployment in the near future.

Analysis shows that young people who have received higher or technical education, although not completely immune, are better protected against the risk of unemployment than others, especially those whose educational standards are below the minimum required to find work in a modern economy. This means that investment in young people's education and continuing training for adults will need to be greater than their numbers would seem to warrant: the problem is then no longer demographic but requires an act of political will.

The female working-age population is also expected to participate increasingly in the labour force. The reason for this is twofold: first, more and more women want (or need) to have a job; second, a growing number of them have the required skills because the level of their education has improved. Thus, rising standards of education and a legitimate desire for financial independence are persuading more and more women to take and, once they are married, to hold on to a job combining, if the circumstances warrant it, their work outside the home with their family commitments. From the demographic point of view, this trend lowers fertility (although female employment is not the only factor) and in any case postpones the age at which women give birth to their first child. Wherever full-time female employment is on the increase, it is unrealistic to expect a high rate of fertility, even if society sets out to ease the situation of working mothers.

In fact, increased female employment is actually beneficial to social security systems since married women who hold jobs pay contributions instead of merely being "protected", for sickness or maternity, through their contribution-paying husbands. However, by contributing, women qualify for future pensions in their own right, whereas those who do not work have to rely on their husbands' pensions and then, when widowed (which statistically is almost a certainty), on a survivor's pension to which they have not contributed financially. To see in increased female employment a remedy for the ageing of the working population is to lose sight of the fact that it will in time increase the number and proportion of pensioners.

THE DEBIT SIDE: BENEFICIARIES

Families and young people

In a study like this, where the accent is on demographic trends, the family must of course be considered the prime target for state intervention and social protection, particularly at a time when, because of low fertility, the population is ageing.

The provision of cash benefits for families (defined as households with young children) or the granting of tax exemptions reflect two different and sometimes conflicting approaches. On the one hand, in the interests of social justice, society tries to ensure that the arrival and continuing presence of children does not penalise families too much, materially speaking. On the other, by regulating the amount of family allowances and the qualifying conditions, society can encourage couples to have children, if possible more than two. This objective may even be carried so far that it discriminates against the first child, whose birth is considered to be "natural", and gives an advantage to the third and any subsequent children, whose arrival is not at all certain although indispensable if the country's population is to be maintained or even increased. Neither of these two policies has quite achieved its objective since allowances, even when the amounts are increased, are far from offsetting the loss of revenue combined with an increase in family size, or the higher cost of maintaining an additional family member, especially when such allowances are not geared to the earnings of the head of the household. Moreover, aid in the form of services (often greatly appreciated by the beneficiaries who, incidentally cannot always afford to pay for such services out of the allowances they receive) is often inadequate or unsuitable (when crèches, for instance, do not always meet the needs of their users).

The amount of family assistance is influenced more by the policies adopted in the field than by the size and structure of the population or, to be more precise, by the number and proportion of children. Political considerations may result in more emphasis being placed on other branches of social security or other items in the social budget.

It would indeed be artificial to consider cash family allowances in isolation from other social measures in favour of families and young people: to do so would be to ignore much more costly benefits such as health, education and housing and help for non-working mothers. While the number of young children is falling there may be an increase in the number of school-age children or of young adults, i.e. those who are particularly concerned by the question of whether or not to start a family or by the presence of young children under their roof.

It would, therefore, be a mistake to conclude that a fall in the birth rate immediately and automatically leads to a drop in expenditure on family welfare. At the same time, it was important to point out in this study that, by adopting certain diversified and co-ordinated measures, the State and social security can help to halt the fertility decline or even reverse the trend. But such policies are both complex and costly, and their implementation can only be achieved as a result of a deliberate political choice.

Pensioners and older beneficiaries

As the result of considerable social progress, pensions provide for former workers and their beneficiaries a substitute income which replaces or sometimes complements the income derived from an occupational activity. To say that social security covers the *risk* of old age is not quite correct in that, with longer life expectancy, old age is no longer just a probability but almost a certainty for the great majority of Europe's inhabitants. What does remain is the need for a replacement income since, for wage earners in particular, after a certain age the older the worker gets the less it is possible, physiologically speaking, to work. As long as society failed to recognise this need (i.e. as late as the beginning of the present century), abject poverty was usually the fate of those who lived longer than the average.

Whatever the system adopted and whatever the methods of financing, retirement pensions can be looked on as a deduction levied on the output of the working population. The resources thus obtained are not "frozen" but "transferred", in that the beneficiaries continue to be consumers and sometimes even savers. As consumers, they provide an outlet for the goods and services produced by the national economy, even though their consumption does not follow quite the same pattern as that of their juniors or that of young people. As savers, they participate in the overall investment process, again to the advantage of the country's economy.

There is a close and basic link between the number of persons in employment and the number of pensioners. In other words, a country in which the dependency ratio is high because of the ageing of its population cannot be as generous to its retired workers as one with a similar level of development but with a younger population.

Thus, when the number of pensioners increases more rapidly than the number of people of working age, it is logical to expect some difficulty in financing pension schemes (although there is no need to be over-pessimistic), whatever the political or economic system in force and whatever the pensions machinery in operation: this latter may in fact be so complicated that its workings can often mask the basic problems.

But are demographic factors the only ones that need to be taken into account?

To be sure, the increase in absolute numbers and in the proportion of older persons is a demographic phenomenon, as is the lengthening of retired life in relation to working life. But other factors also play their part, such as the maturing of pension schemes, the extension of coverage to large groups of the population, improved coverage of claimants (widows in particular), and subsidisation of pension schemes with a diminishing number of contributors (in branches which are losing ground as a result of technological change). The financial pressure on all systems may also be increased by widespread and lasting unemployment (by whatever name it is known). The rules applied in indexing the pensions of the already retired can also affect financing; often it is necessary to revoke socially generous and justified provisions (the indexing of pensions to wages) and to limit increases to rises in the price index, with a shorter or longer time-lag.

In countries with no national pension system or where the systems in operation are strictly occupational, it is also necessary to grant welfare benefits to older persons who do not qualify for a pension at all, or who only qualify for a partial pension, when their own resources are insufficient for their needs. Such allowances are not dependent upon the prior payment of contributions; they are financed, directly or indirectly, from taxation even though they may in fact be transmitted via pension funds. Although, from the legal point of view, they differ considerably from retirement pensions, from a financial point of view they too are transfers designed to prevent needy old people from falling below the poverty line.

Health expenditure

Protection of the population against the risk of illness varies widely from country to country, especially when taken in its broadest sense, i.e. to include not only reimbursement of hospital and medical expenses as such, but also the cost of prevention and compensation for loss of earnings.

Individual medical expenditure is closely bound up with age. Fairly high during the first year of life (to which must be added the antenatal period), it falls, then rises again, increasing rapidly after the age of 60. In spite of the relatively small numbers involved, the percentage of total medical expenditure occasioned by older persons is fairly high. It is difficult to make international comparisons since there is no guarantee that the level, quality, nature and volume of care are identical from one country to another: it is, however, clear that the percentage of old people in the population is significant in that their share in the growth of medical expenditure is more than proportionate to their numbers.

The level of expenditure is, however, no proof that the needs of older people are today covered to the same extent as those of younger ones: this inadequacy often has tragic consequences for those who are both very old and dependent. In other words, health expenditure related to the presence of a high proportion of older persons (the very old in particular) would immediately rise if their needs were better catered for. It can be seen, then, that at equivalent levels of development, the health needs of an "aged" population can be proportionately more expensive than those of a younger population.

More generally speaking, the links between population trends and health costs are hardly ever straightforward. A fall in the birth rate brings down medical expenditure to begin with, but later on the cost increases as more care is taken to bring down sickness and mortality rates among mothers and infants. The length of hospital stays, instead of reflecting the poor state of health of the elderly, could well be a sign that other forms of accommodation and care are lacking.

In short, health and its protection cannot be measured merely by the amount of medical expenditure, individual or collective.

Inasmuch as the resources come from the socially insured (as contributors or as producers), it goes without saying that any fall in output or productivity caused directly by sickness or accidents (and the ensuing absence from work), and by unemployment, places a heavy burden on finances. Any effective measures to improve the health of the working population may be regarded in the same light as the introduction of shorter working hours, and a reduction in the arduousness of work and the number of hazardous jobs.

Increased longevity itself poses certain problems in that it is not always accompanied by improvements in the quality of life: nowadays it is possible to live a long while in a poor state of health. This prolongation of life is, however, not the same for both sexes or for all social and occupational groups.

The optimum use of resources—which will always be limited—may be adversely affected by especially high expenditure in regions where ageing of the local population is more marked than in others. Economies of scale can help city-dwellers, but are not much use to older country-dwellers, especially those living in widely dispersed communities situated far from well-equipped and well-staffed centres. Appropriate maps could be used to show the areas with a high incidence of ageing and an accumulation of handicaps.

It is clear that in any case the consequences for the ageing European populations in terms of health raise two questions for social security, as they do for any collective coverage of expenditure. First, is it possible to restructure the provision of care to cater to the specific needs of older people, thereby enabling them to enjoy, in the same way as other social groups, the best possible state of health. Second, how can the additional cost which would inevitably result from such restructuring best be met in an overall economic climate where pessimism is likely to remain the order of the day?

The aim of this study was not to provide ready-made answers to such fundamental questions as these, but simply to throw some light on two aspects of the problems involved in providing health care for societies where both the numbers and the proportions of older people are increasing: adjustment is necessary and a rise in costs inevitable. It is, of course, for the governments and peoples of Europe to seek solutions compatible with both moral and financial necessities, so that the health of the elderly is not sacrificed on the altar of economic rationalism as applied to social security.

STATISTICAL APPENDIX

Tables A.1–A.5 in this appendix are based on data extracted from the following sources: United Nations: *World population prospects: Estimates and projections as assessed in 1984* (New York, 1986); idem: *Global estimates and projections by sex and age: The 1984 assessment* (New York, 1987).

The countries in these tables are listed within groupings (see Chapter 1) in geographical order, from north to south.

Table A.2. Evolution of the population, overall and by age group, 1985–2025 (numbers in thousands)

Age groups	0–4			5–14			15–19			20–59		
Group/ Country	1985	2000	2025	1985	2000	2025	1985	2000	2025	1985	2000	2025
EEC												
Denmark	276	261	219	681	557	444	392	282	232	2 741	2 939	2 400
Netherlands	894	786	762	1 950	1 700	1 461	1 232	906	722	8 031	8 880	7 324
Belgium	612	573	613	1 263	1 177	1 210	729	619	598	5 399	5 547	4 929
Luxembourg	21	19	19	43	39	37	27	21	18	207	204	168
Germany, Fed. Rep of	3 047	3 016	2 973	6 309	6 455	5 605	4 857	3 036	2 609	34 477	32 719	25 658
United Kingdom	3 727	3 488	3 474	7 216	7 192	6 854	4 425	3 686	3 297	29 122	30 527	27 908
Ireland	368	395	369	699	793	747	340	367	377	1 681	2 232	2 929
France	3 872	3 552	3 500	7 783	7 325	6 908	4 165	3 855	3 419	29 148	31 319	29 473
Portugal	836	832	790	1 676	1 675	1 588	867	824	795	5 281	6 017	6 431
Spain	2 723	3 109	2 925	6 642	5 953	5 766	3 288	2 712	2 950	19 831	22 649	24 270
Italy	3 150	3 638	3 379	7 969	6 887	6 301	4 560	3 138	3 174	30 937	32 124	28 976
Greece	710	694	666	1 418	1 407	1 342	777	706	672	5 212	5 361	5 539
Total	20 236	20 363	19 689	43 649	41 160	38 263	25 659	20 152	18 863	172 067	180 618	166 005
Northern Europe												
Iceland	23	19	18	42	40	37	21	23	19	124	151	158
Norway	258	234	245	576	490	475	334	263	231	2 101	2 399	2 157
Sweden	476	411	419	1 047	842	800	601	485	409	4 326	4 595	3 838
Finland	321	282	273	622	606	550	359	326	279	2 748	2 879	2 495
Total	1 078	946	955	2 287	1 978	1 862	1 315	1 097	938	9 299	10 024	8 648
Alpine Europe												
Switzerland	361	308	301	763	675	573	483	360	281	3 543	3 572	2 797
Austria	463	423	405	930	913	828	607	461	406	4 017	4 180	3 635
Total	824	731	706	1 693	1 588	1 401	1 090	821	687	7 560	7 752	6 432
Adriatic Europe												
Yugoslavia	1 803	1 702	1 698	3 711	3 457	3 318	1 802	1 791	1 667	12 909	13 762	13 812
Albania	382	431	500	698	854	941	316	378	447	1 441	2 072	3 039
Total	2 185	2 133	2 198	4 409	4 311	4 259	2 118	2 169	2 114	14 350	15 834	16 841
Mediterranean island countries												
Malta	32	29	29	59	60	60	26	32	30	213	235	231
Cyprus	66	56	63	103	120	128	49	66	64	361	411	449
Total	98	85	92	162	180	188	75	98	94	574	646	1 380
Eastern Europe												
German Dem. Rep.	1 169	1 059	1 098	2 060	2 259	2 242	1 223	1 185	1 128	9 285	9 155	8 675
Poland	3 300	2 924	3 010	6 093	5 916	5 941	2 516	3 286	3 027	20 140	21 996	23 166
Czechoslavia	1 171	1 239	1 235	2 639	2 292	2 378	1 068	1 167	1 194	8 161	9 167	9 449
Hungary	676	685	649	1 635	1 184	1 242	710	673	635	5 729	6 034	5 505
Romania	1 908	2 038	2 145	3 896	3 936	4 180	2 001	1 891	2 033	11 940	13 184	15 389
Bulgaria	690	651	673	1 334	1 317	1 340	623	686	669	4 856	4 953	5 153
Total	8 914	8 596	8 810	17 657	16 904	17 323	8 141	8 888	8 686	60 111	64 489	67 337
USSR	25 047	24 252	27 250	44 171	49 794	54 083	20 230	24 852	26 627	1 52 601	1 60 716	1 84 199
Turkey	6 364	7 039	7 964	11 559	13 813	15 488	5 401	6 197	7 364	22 812	32 911	53 386

60 and over			of which: 65 and over			of which: 80 and over			Total			Median age (years)		
1985	2000	2025	1985	2000	2025	1985	2000	2025	1985	2000	2025	1985	2000	2025
1 032	1 043	1 395	764	781	1 043.	162	195	235	5 122	5 082	4 690	35.9	39.6	46.4
2 393	2 810	4 422	1 709	2 067	3 258	347	423	614	14 500	15 082	14 691	33.0	38.7	46.2
1 900	2 095	2 704	1 330	1 580	1 986	287	296	387	9 903	10 011	10 054	35.1	38.9	42.0
65	75	97	46	54	72	8	9	14	363	358	339	35.9	40.3	44.0
12 187	14 258	16 645	8 813	9 942	12 018	1 951	1 980	2 855	60 877	59 484	53 490	37.7	41.1	45.9
11 635	11 461	14 386	8 465	8 640	10 437	1 732	2 011	2 211	56 125	56 354	55 919	35.4	37.7	41.1
520	533	904	374	393	618	65	80	103	3 608	4 320	5 326	26.4	28.7	34.9
9 653	11 111	15 131	6 749	8 396	11 273	1 741	1 502	2 111	54 621	57 162	58 431	33.6	37.3	41.6
1 552	1 863	2 730	1 075	1 377	1 933	158	217	336	10 212	11 211	12 334	30.1	33.7	38.4
6 058	7 814	10 072	4 274	5 751	7 217	730	1 022	1 491	38 542	42 237	45 983	31.2	34.2	38.8
10 684	12 855	15 348	7 442	9 412	11 222	1 436	1 703	2 485	57 300	58 642	57 178	35.5	38.5	43.0
1 761	2 269	2 570	1 298	1 682	1 921	261	325	457	9 878	10 437	10 789	34.8	36.7	39.7
59 440	68 187	86 404	42 339	50 075	62 998	8 876	9 763	13 299	321 051	330 380	329 224			
33	40	72	24	31	52	5	7	10	243	273	304	28.1	33.4	40.5
873	829	1 153	644	644	862	133	169	175	4 142	4 215	4 261	34.5	38.1	43.6
1 901	1 833	2 241	1 416	1 405	1 709	295	365	404	8 351	8 166	7 707	37.5	40.6	45.1
841	962	1 397	600	711	1 050	108	150	203	4 891	5 055	4 994	34.6	39.0	42.9
3 748	3 664	4 863	2 684	2 792	3 673	541	691	792	17 627	17 709	17 266			
1 224	1 426	1 832	894	1 058	1 379	199	232	329	6 374	6 341	5 784	36.5	41.1	46.8
1 485	1 540	2 005	1 060	1 136	1 434	228	227	311	7 502	7 517	7 279	35.3	38.5	43.0
2 709	2 966	3 837	1 954	2 194	2 813	427	459	640	13 876	13 858	13 063			
2 928	4 494	6 261	1 905	3 185	4 638	310	388	840	23 153	25 206	26 756	31.4	35.5	39.7
213	367	845	150	243	568	21	35	89	3 050	4 102	5 772	22.1	25.4	31.6
3 141	4 861	7 106	2 055	3 428	5 206	331	423	929	26 203	29 308	32 528			
53	62	109	36	43	81	7	8	13	383	418	459	31.3	35.6	38.8
90	109	198	66	75	·146	11	14	23	669	762	902	29.6	33.6	36.7
143	171	307	102	118	227	18	22	36	1 072	1 180	1 361			
3 029	3 491	4 427	2 228	2 351	3 157	508	403	663	16 766	17 149	17 570	34.5	37.9	39.8
5 138	6 694	10 142	3 484	4 897	7 736	650	764	1 243	37 187	40 816	45 286	30.9	34.5	38.1
2 540	2 716	3 901	1 709	2 027	2 945	322	323	518	15 579	16 581	18 157	32.6	34.6	37.8
1 947	2 138	2 567	1 333	1 597	2 017	240	255	391	10 697	10 714	10 598	35.0	38.0	41.1
3 272	4 522	5 500	2 155	3 193	4 252	348	412	793	23 017	25 571	29 247	31.5	32.7	35.6
1 568	1 928	2 235	1 024	1 441	1 686	167	210	347	9 071	9 535	10 070	34.9	36.4	38.0
17 494	21 489	28 772	11 933	15 506	21 793	2 235	2 367	3 955	112 317	120 366	130 928			
36 569	55 122	76 075	25 974	37 303	54 641	4 610	5 706	9 966	278 618	314 736	368 234	30.3	33.7	35.5
3 153	5 391	11 810	2 093	3 615	7 723	260	382	1 043	49 289	65 351	91 925	21.4	25.0	30.8

Table A.3. Young people (0–19 years): Numbers in thousands and rate of change, 1985–2025 (index: 1985 = 100)

Group/country	Age group 0–4 years No.			Index		Age group 5–14 years No.			Index		Age group 15–19 years No.			Index	
	1985	2000	2025	2000	2025	1985	2000	2025	2000	2025	1985	2000	2025	2000	2025
EEC															
Denmark	276	261	219	95	79	681	557	444	82	65	392	282	232	72	59
Netherlands	894	786	762	88	85	1 955	1 700	1 461	87	75	1 232	906	722	74	59
Belgium	612	573	613	94	100	1 263	1 177	1 210	93	96	729	619	598	85	82
Luxembourg	21	19	19	90	90	43	39	37	91	86	27	21	18	78	67
Germany, Fed. Rep. of	3 047	3 016	2 973	99	98	6 209	6 455	5 605	104	90	4 857	3 036	2 609	63	54
United Kingdom	3 727	3 488	3 474	94	93	7 316	7 192	6 854	98	94	4 425	3 686	3 297	83	75
Ireland	368	395	369	107	100	699	793	747	113	107	340	367	377	108	111
France	3 872	3 552	3 500	92	90	7 783	7 325	6 908	94	89	4 165	3 855	3 419	93	82
Portugal	836	832	790	100	94	1 676	1 675	1 588	100	95	867	824	795	95	92
Spain	2 723	3 109	2 925	114	107	6 642	5 953	5 766	90	87	3 288	2 712	2 950	82	90
Italy	3 150	3 638	3 379	115	107	7 969	6 887	6 301	86	79	4 560	3 138	3 174	69	70
Greece	710	694	666	98	93	1 418	1 407	1 342	99	95	777	706	672	91	86
Total	20 236	20 363	19 689	101	97	43 654	41 160	38 263	94	88	25 659	20 152	18 863	79	74
Northern Europe															
Iceland	23	19	18	83	78	42	40	37	95	88	21	23	19	110	90
Norway	258	234	245	91	95	576	492	475	85	82	334	263	231	79	69
Sweden	476	411	419	86	88	1 047	842	800	80	76	601	485	409	81	68
Finland	321	282	273	88	85	621	606	550	98	89	359	326	279	91	78
Total	1 078	946	955	88	89	2 286	1 980	1 862	87	81	1 315	1 097	938	83	71

Alpine Europe															
Switzerland	361	308	301	85	83	763	675	573	88	75	483	360	281	75	58
Austria	463	423	405	91	87	930	913	828	98	89	607	461	406	76	67
Total	824	731	706	89	86	1 693	1 588	1 401	94	83	1 090	821	687	75	63
Adriatic Europe															
Yugoslavia	1 803	1 702	1 698	94	94	3 711	3 457	3 318	93	89	1 802	1 791	1 667	99	93
Albania	382	431	500	113	131	698	854	941	122	134	316	378	447	120	141
Total	2 185	2 133	2 198	98	101	4 409	4 311	4 259	98	97	2 118	2 169	2 114	102	100
Mediterranean island countries															
Malta	32	29	29	91	91	59	60	60	102	102	26	32	30	123	115
Cyprus	66	56	63	85	95	103	120	128	117	124	49	66	64	135	131
Total	98	85	92	87	108	162	180	188	111	116	75	98	94	131	125
Eastern Europe															
German Dem. Rep.	1 169	1 059	1 098	91	94	2 060	2 259	2 242	110	109	1 223	1 185	1 128	97	92
Poland	3 300	2 924	3 010	89	91	6 193	5 916	5 941	96	96	2 516	3 286	3 027	131	120
Czechoslovakia	1 171	1 239	1 235	106	106	2 639	2 292	2 378	87	90	1 068	1 167	1 194	109	112
Hungary	676	685	649	101	96	1 635	1 254	1 342	77	82	710	673	635	95	89
Romania	1 908	2 038	2 145	107	112	3 896	3 936	4 180	101	107	2 001	1 891	2 033	95	102
Bulgaria	690	651	673	94	98	1 334	1 317	1 340	99	100	623	686	669	110	107
Total	8 914	8 596	8 810	96	99	17 757	16 974	17 423	96	98	8 141	8 888	8 686	109	107
USSR	25 047	24 252	27 250	97	109	44 171	49 794	54 083	113	122	20 230	24 852	26 627	123	132
Turkey	6 364	7 039	7 964	111	125	11 559	13 813	15 488	119	134	5 401	6 197	7 364	115	136

Table A.4. Working-age population (20–59 years): Numbers in thousands and rate of change, 1985–2025 (index: 1985=100)

| Group/country | Age group 20–39 years | | | | | Age group 40–59 years | | | | | Ratio 40–59/20–39 | | | | |
| | No. | | | Index | | No. | | | Index | | % | | | Index | |
	1985	2000	2025	2000	2025	1985	2000	2025	2000	2025	1985	2000	2025	2000	2025
EEC															
Denmark	1 549	1 476	1 083	95	70	1 190	1 464	1 317	123	111	76.8	99.2	121.6	129	158
Netherlands	4 832	4 478	3 279	93	68	3 197	4 400	4 046	138	122	66.2	98.3	123.4	148	186
Belgium	3 059	2 804	2 364	92	77	2 339	2 741	2 566	117	110	76.5	97.8	108.5	128	142
Luxembourg	113	98	77	87	68	95	105	91	111	96	84.1	107.1	118.2	127	141
Germany, Fed. Rep. of	18 060	16 210	12 064	90	68	16 416	16 507	13 594	101	83	90.9	101.8	112.7	112	124
United Kingdom	16 448	15 799	13 586	96	82	12 674	14 729	14 321	116	113	77.1	93.2	105.4	121	137
Ireland	1 052	1 351	1 566	124	143	631	881	1 361	140	216	60.0	65.2	86.9	108	145
France	16 933	16 107	14 203	95	84	12 216	15 211	15 269	125	125	72.1	94.4	107.5	131	149
Portugal	3 124	3 367	3 255	108	104	2 156	2 648	3 177	123	147	69.0	78.7	97.6	114	141
Spain	11 014	13 003	12 054	118	109	8 820	9 646	12 216	109	101	80.1	74.2	101.3	93	126
Italy	16 653	16 981	13 856	103	84	14 285	15 142	15 120	106	106	85.8	89.2	109.1	104	127
Greece	2 715	2 885	2 754	106	101	2 497	2 475	2 786	99	112	92.0	85.8	101.2	93	110
Total	95 552	94 559	80 441	99	84	76 516	85 949	85 864	112	112	80.1	90.9	106.8	114	133
Northern Europe															
Iceland	78	85	75	109	96	45	67	87	149	193	57.7	78.8	116.0	137	201
Norway	1 246	1 241	984	100	79	853	1 159	1 172	136	137	68.5	93.3	119.1	136	174
Sweden	2 386	2 278	1 726	116	72	1 941	2 317	2 114	119	109	81.4	101.7	122.5	125	150
Finland	1 619	1 389	1 202	86	74	1 130	1 491	1 293	132	114	69.8	107.3	107.6	154	154
Total	5 329	4 993	3 987	94	75	3 969	5 034	4 666	127	118	74.5	100.8	117.0	135	154

Alpine Europe															
Switzerland	1933	1731	1255	90	65	1611	1842	1541	114	96	83.3	106.4	122.8	128	147
Austria	2230	2157	1726	97	77	1787	2022	1911	113	107	80.1	93.7	111.7	117	138
Total	4163	3888	2981	93	72	3398	3864	3452	114	102	81.6	99.4	105.8	122	142
Adriatic Europe															
Yugoslavia	7282	7283	6809	100	94	5629	6479	7006	115	124	77.3	89.0	102.9	116	133
Albania	950	1307	1702	138	179	492	765	1338	155	272	51.8	58.5	78.6	113	152
Total	8232	8590	8511	104	103	6121	7244	8344	118	136	74.4	84.3	98.0	113	132
Mediterranean island countries															
Malta	132	116	118	88	89	79	120	114	152	144	59.9	103.5	96.6	173	162
Cyprus	228	209	236	92	104	132	200	212	152	161	57.9	95.7	89.8	165	155
Total	360	325	354	90	98	211	320	326	152	159	58.6	98.5	94.9	168	162
Eastern Europe															
German Dem. Rep.	4932	4660	4366	95	89	4332	4495	4310	104	100	87.8	95.5	98.7	109	112
Poland	12151	11253	11781	86	97	7987	10744	11385	135	143	65.7	95.5	96.6	145	147
Czechoslovakia	4721	4762	4758	101	101	3442	4407	4691	128	136	72.9	92.6	98.6	127	135
Hungary	3087	2962	2629	96	85	2643	2973	2877	112	109	85.6	100.4	109.4	117	128
Romania	6404	7240	7950	113	124	5534	5945	7436	107	134	86.4	82.1	93.5	95	108
Bulgaria	2560	2554	.2610	100	102	2297	2399	2541	104	111	89.7	93.0	97.4	105	109
Total	33855	33431	34096	99	101	26235	30963	33240	118	127	77.5	92.6	97.5	119	126
USSR	86834	87607	98516	101	113	65767	73110	85681	111	130	75.7	83.5	87.0	110	115
Turkey	14864	21290	27541	143	185	7947	11622	21754	146	274	53.5	54.6	79.0	102	148

Table A.5. Older persons (65 years and over): Numbers in thousands and rate of change, 1985–2025 (index: 1985 = 100)

| Group/country | Age group 65–79 years | | | | | Age group 80 and over | | | | | Ratio 80+/65–79 | | | | |
| | No. | | | Index | | No. | | | Index | | % | | | Index | |
	1985	2000	2025	2000	2025	1985	2000	2025	2000	2025	1985	2000	2025	2000	2025
EEC															
Denmark	601	585	808	98	135	162	195	235	120	145	27.0	33.3	29.1	123	108
Netherlands	1 362	1 645	2 624	121	193	347	423	614	122	177	25.5	25.7	23.4	103	92
Belgium	773	1 284	1 601	166	207	287	296	387	103	135	37.1	23.1	24.2	62	65
Luxembourg	38	46	58	121	153	8	9	14	113	175	21.1	19.6	24.1	93	114
Germany, Fed. Rep. of	6 861	7 962	9 162	116	134	1 951	1 980	2 855	102	146	28.4	24.9	31.2	88	110
United Kingdom	6 734	6 629	8 226	98	122	1 732	2 011	2 211	116	128	25.7	30.3	26.1	118	105
Ireland	310	313	515	110	166	65	80	101	123	155	21.0	25.6	19.6	122	93
France	5 007	6 893	9 162	138	183	1 741	1 502	2 111	86	121	34.8	21.5	23.0	62	66
Portugal	919	1 160	1 597	126	174	156	217	336	139	215	17.0	18.7	36.5	110	215
Spain	3 544	4 728	5 726	133	161	730	1 022	1 491	140	204	20.6	21.6	26.0	105	126
Italy	6 007	7 709	8 734	128	146	1 438	1 703	2 405	118	167	24.0	22.1	27.5	92	115
Greece	1 038	1 357	1 465	131	141	261	325	457	125	175	25.1	23.9	31.2	95	124
Total	33 194	34 101	49 678	103	150	8 878	9 763	13 217	110	149	26.8	28.6	26.6	107	99
Northern Europe															
Iceland	19	23	42	121	221	5	7	10	140	200	26.3	30.4	23.8	116	90
Norway	511	476	657	93	134	133	169	175	127	132	26.0	35.5	25.5	137	98
Sweden	1 100	1 039	1 364	94	124	295	365	404	124	137	26.8	35.1	29.6	131	110
Finland	492	561	847	114	172	108	150	203	139	188	22.0	26.7	24.0	121	109
Total	2 122	2 099	2 910	99	137	541	691	792	128	146	25.5	32.9	27.2	129	107

Alpine Europe															
Switzerland	695	826	1 049	119	151	199	232	329	117	165	28.6	28.1	31.4	98	109
Austria	831	910	1 114	110	134	228	227	311	100	136	27.4	24.9	27.9	91	101
Total	1 526	1 736	2 163	114	142	427	459	640	107	150	28.0	26.4	29.6	94	106
Adriatic Europe															
Yugoslavia	1 595	2 797	3 598	175	226	310	388	840	125	271	19.4	13.9	23.3	72	120
Albania	129	207	479	160	371	21	35	89	167	424	16.3	16.9	18.6	104	114
Total	1 724	3 004	4 077	174	236	331	423	929	128	281	19.2	14.1	22.8	73	119
Mediterranean island countries															
Malta	29	35	68	121	234	7	8	13	114	186	24.1	22.9	19.1	95	79
Cyprus	54	60	123	111	228	11	14	23	127	209	20.4	23.3	18.7	114	92
Total	83	95	191	114	230	18	22	36	122	200	21.7	23.2	18.8	107	87
Eastern Europe															
German Dem. Rep.	1 719	1 948	1 495	113	87	508	403	663	79	131	29.6	20.7	44.3	70	150
Poland	2 834	4 133	6 493	146	229	650	764	1 243	118	191	22.9	18.3	19.1	80	83
Czechoslovakia	1 387	1 704	2 427	123	175	322	323	518	100	161	23.2	19.0	21.3	82	92
Hungary	1 093	1 341	1 626	123	149	240	255	391	106	163	22.0	19.0	25.6	86	116
Romania	1 807	1 781	3 459	99	191	348	412	793	118	228	19.3	23.1	22.9	120	119
Bulgaria	857	1 231	1 339	144	156	167	210	347	126	208	19.5	17.1	25.9	88	133
Total	9 697	12 138	16 839	125	174	2 235	2 367	3 955	106	177	23.1	19.5	23.5	84	102
USSR	21 364	31 597	44 675	148	209	4 610	5 706	9 966	124	216	21.6	18.1	22.3	84	103
Turkey	1 833	3 232	6 681	176	364	260	382	1 043	147	401	14.2	11.8	15.6	83	110

Table A.6. Average labour force participation rates of the population aged 55 and over in European subregions, 1950–85

Subregion/age group	1950 Male	1950 Female	1950 Total	1960 Male	1960 Female	1960 Total	1970 Male	1970 Female	1970 Total	1980 Male	1980 Female	1980 Total	1985 Male	1985 Female	1985 Total
Eastern Europe															
55–59	93.90	49.40	68.65	91.00	52.85	70.60	88.45	53.65	69.30	81.05	47.65	62.60	80.55	45.95	62.15
60–64	81.50	39.65	57.45	75.55	38.00	54.40	70.45	34.20	50.50	47.55	24.55	34.60	45.80	22.35	32.60
65+	49.50	21.30	33.40	44.30	17.75	28.40	40.90	15.85	25.95	18.80	9.45	13.15	16.75	8.05	11.40
Average 55+	70.9	34.1	49.8	67.5	32.7	47.6	61.5	29.5	43.02	41.4	20.5	29.7	42.8	25.5	29.8
Northern Europe															
55–59	96.40	26.65	58.60	94.55	34.85	63.35	92.20	44.55	67.55	89.60	55.30	71.90	89.20	54.60	71.50
60–64	91.45	17.60	50.90	85.80	20.15	49.75	76.65	23.55	49.90	71.70	26.75	47.95	71.15	25.85	47.30
65+	36.65	7.50	19.95	29.10	6.15	15.40	20.90	4.95	11.30	12.35	4.20	7.45	11.70	3.60	6.85
Average 55+	65.6	14.6	37.1	61.8	16.3	36.1	55.0	17.9	34.0	44.9	19.1	30.2	43.7	17.6	28.9
Southern Europe[1]															
55–59	90.35	17.53	50.15	88.35	18.75	51.80	80.95	19.10	48.20	72.00	19.45	43.95	71.65	18.85	44.00
60–64	80.10	14.70	43.75	72.25	15.05	40.80	59.75	14.25	35.50	46.90	12.30	28.00	44.05	11.45	26.35
65+	55.55	9.30	29.15	42.10	8.35	22.45	20.05	6.00	14.35	14.70	3.75	8.30	13.00	3.15	7.20
Average 55+	71.3	12.8	38.4	63.3	12.6	35.0	50.0	11.2	28.3	36.5	9.1	27.10	36.8	8.8	21.1

Western Europe															
55–59	87.40	32.10	56.00	85.95	33.50	58.25	84.30	35.10	57.15	78.10	35.95	54.85	78.10	35.50	56.00
60–64	78.10	26.85	49.15	70.75	23.35	44.15	63.00	20.40	39.30	41.75	15.10	26.70	40.20	14.75	25.90
65+	32.20	11.35	20.25	22.40	8.15	13.80	15.00	5.60	9.30	5.70	2.90	3.95	5.40	2.50	3.55
Average 55+	57.60	20.4	36.4	53.6	18.2	33.3	44.4	15.4	27.5	31.0	12.0	19.7	33.4	11.8	20.7
USSR															
55–59	89.50	50.90	65.50	83.25	45.65	58.70	79.45	25.35	44.60	78.75	25.00	44.60	77.35	23.95	47.10
60–64	86.50	42.60	59.05	52.50	35.80	41.50	31.80	10.45	18.05	30.55	9.65	16.95	29.40	8.85	16.10
65+	49.00	35.00	39.15	39.00	26.80	30.70	12.50	4.05	6.65	10.00	3.00	5.10	8.95	2.55	4.40
Total 55+	71.50	40.9	51.2	57.3	34.3	41.5	38.30	11.5	20.4	32.9	9.2	16.9	39.9	9.7	20.5

[1] Excluding Cyprus and Turkey.

Source: ILO: *Economically active population: Estimates and projections: 1950–2025*, Vol. II (Geneva, 3rd ed., 1986).

Table A.7 First hypothesis: Impact of ageing of populations on medical expenditure,[1] various European countries, 1985, 2000 and 2015

| Country | Per capita medical expenditure (index: Europe = 100) | | | Average annual growth (%)[2] | | | % share of old persons in total medical expenditure | | | | | |
| | | | | | | | Over 65 | | | Over 75 | | |
	1985	2000	2015	1985–2000	2000–2015	1985–2015	1985	2000	2015	1985	2000	2015
Albania	82	83	84	0.28	0.42	0.35	16	20	24	8	9	12
Austria	103	102	102	0.15	0.26	0.21	38	38	42	22	22	24
Belgium	103	103	103	0.20	0.29	0.24	36	39	43	20	22	22
Bulgaria	100	100	98	0.20	0.14	0.17	34	39	40	17	21	22
Czechoslovakia	98	96	95	0.07	0.25	0.16	33	32	38	18	18	18
Denmark	103	103	106	0.25	0.43	0.34	38	38	45	21	22	24
Finland	100	101	105	0.29	0.50	0.39	33	36	45	18	20	22
France	101	100	101	0.17	0.32	0.24	35	37	41	20	21	21
German Democratic Republic	102	102	103	0.22	0.29	0.26	36	39	42	23	19	24
Germany, Federal Republic of	104	106	107	0.37	0.34	0.35	37	42	46	22	22	27
Greece	101	100	97	0.15	0.07	0.11	35	40	39	20	22	23
Hungary	101	100	100	0.19	0.28	0.23	35	37	42	19	20	22

Iceland	95	94	98	0.16	0.51	0.34	30	30	36	16	17	18
Ireland	93	89	88	−0.08	0.21	0.07	31	27	29	17	15	14
Italy	102	103	102	0.28	0.23	0.26	36	40	43	20	22	24
Luxembourg	102	105	106	0.37	0.38	0.37	35	36	46	20	20	24
Netherlands	99	101	105	0.32	0.56	0.44	33	36	44	17	20	22
Norway	103	101	102	0.10	0.33	0.21	40	37	42	22	23	22
Poland	95	95	96	0.20	0.38	0.29	28	33	37	15	17	17
Portugal	95	93	95	0.09	0.39	0.24	30	32	35	15	17	17
Romania	95	95	94	0.24	0.16	0.20	29	35	36	15	17	19
Spain	97	96	94	0.18	0.16	0.17	32	35	36	16	19	19
Sweden	106	106	107	0.19	0.31	0.25	42	41	47	23	25	26
Switzerland	107	113	114	0.58	0.36	0.47	40	46	53	22	26	32
United Kingdom	103	100	100	0.06	0.25	0.16	38	38	41	21	22	22
Yugoslavia	94	95	98	0.28	0.48	0.38	26	35	39	14	17	20
Europe	100	100	100	0.21	0.27	0.24	34	37	41	19	20	22

[1] Calculations based on the following assumptions: United Nations population projections; differential growth rates, by age group, of average medical expenditure are those noted in France (INSEE/CREDES Inquiry, 1980) *and are kept constant over the whole period.*   [2] Growth due to changes in age structure.

Table A.8. Second hypothesis: Impact of ageing of populations on medical expenditure,[1] various European countries, 1985, 2000 and 2015

Country	Per capita medical expenditure (index: Europe = 100)			Average annual growth (%)[2]			% share of old persons in total medical expenditure					
							Over 65			Over 75		
	1985	2000	2015	1985–2000	2000–2015	1985–2015	1985	2000	2015	1985	2000	2015
Albania	80	76	73	0.27	0.95	0.61	18	27	37	9	12	18
Austria	103	103	103	0.55	1.24	0.89	40	48	59	24	27	33
Belgium	103	103	105	0.59	1.35	0.97	39	49	60	21	27	32
Bulgaria	100	100	98	0.56	1.13	0.84	36	48	58	18	25	32
Czechoslovakia	97	93	92	0.27	1.18	0.72	35	41	54	19	22	26
Denmark	103	105	108	0.71	1.46	1.08	41	48	63	22	28	34
Finland	100	101	107	0.65	1.64	1.14	36	45	62	19	25	30
France	101	99	102	0.51	1.39	0.95	37	46	59	21	26	31
German Democratic Republic	103	103	103	0.64	1.20	0.92	39	49	59	24	24	33
Germany, Federal Republic of	104	109	110	0.89	1.33	1.11	39	51	63	23	27	37
Greece	101	102	98	0.61	0.98	0.79	37	50	57	21	27	34
Hungary	101	99	101	0.51	1.32	0.91	37	46	59	20	25	31

Iceland	94	91	94	0.34	1.47	0.90	32	39	53	17	22	27
Ireland	92	85	79	0.05	0.74	0.39	33	36	44	18	20	22
Italy	102	105	105	0.76	1.25	1.01	38	50	61	21	28	36
Luxembourg	102	106	110	0.83	1.47	1.15	38	49	63	21	24	34
Netherlands	99	101	107	0.71	1.65	1.18	35	45	61	19	25	31
Norway	104	102	104	0.51	1.31	0.91	42	47	60	23	30	32
Poland	94	92	95	0.41	1.42	0.91	30	42	54	16	22	26
Portugal	95	91	90	0.30	1.20	0.75	32	42	51	16	21	26
Romania	94	94	90	0.53	0.99	0.76	31	44	53	16	21	28
Spain	96	95	92	0.49	0.98	0.74	34	44	53	17	24	30
Sweden	107	109	111	0.71	1.34	1.03	44	51	64	25	31	36
Switzerland	107	118	125	1.23	1.64	1.43	42	56	70	23	32	43
United Kingdom	103	101	100	0.46	1.17	0.81	41	47	58	22	27	32
Yugoslavia	93	93	97	0.56	1.49	1.03	28	44	56	15	20	29
Europe	100	100	100	0.58	1.23	0.91	37	47	58	20	25	32

[1] Calculations based on the following assumptions: United Nations population projections; differential growth rates, by age group, of average medical expenditure *vary according to age groups* and are calculated to correspond with those observed in France between 1970 and 1980, assuming that the growth rate for the total population is zero at the beginning of the period. [2] Growth due to changes in age structure.

187